Plant-Based Diet Cookbook for Beginners

A Complete Meal Prep Guide with Delicious, Quick & Easy Plant-Based Diet Recipes to Reset & Energize Your Body and Live a Healthy Lifestyle

contained within this document, including, but not limited to, — errors, omissions, or inaccuracies.

Table of Content

Chapter 4: Plant-Based Lunch Recipes..........107

Kaput Tabbouleh Salad

Chapter 5: Plant-Based Snacks Recipes........138

Smoky Pinto Bean Tostadas

Vegetarian Cheese Popcorn

Corn Salsa with Black Eyed Peas Cake

Banh Mi Pizza

Cauliflower with Sichuan Tofu

Lentil-Tahini Burgers Spicy

Easy Gregory Burger

Best Vegan Gluten-Free Mac 'N' Cheese

Sprouted Lentils

Jamaican Jerk Grilled Eggplant

Noodle-Free Pad Thai

Baked Quinoa Black Beans Fruit Fil Quinoa

Moroccan Lentil-Stuffed Eggplant

Garlic And White Wine Paste

Baked Quinoa Black Beans Fruit Fil Quinoa

Thai Yellow Coconut Curry Mango

The best vegetarian 'full PORK' Sandwich!

The Best Vegetarian 'Full Pork' Sandwich

Crispy Gluten-Free Eggplant Parmesan

Garlic Sandwich Potato Noodle Pasta Unripe

Collard Green Spring Rolls + Sunbutter Dipping Saving

Blundered Ward Veggies

Mediterranean Baked Sweet Potatoes

Butternut Squash Veggie Pizza

Introduction

Congratulations on purchasing *Plant-Based Diet Cookbook for Beginners* and thank you for doing so.

A Plant-Based weight loss plan is a diet that includes vegetables, grains, nuts, seeds, legumes, and fruits from plant-derived food or entirely with more and few or no animal products. A plant-based diet is no longer necessarily vegetarian. The use of the phrase plant-based has been modified over time, and the example phrase "plant-based diet" can be traced back to being used to refer to vegetarian diets, including any food from animal sources No, vegan diets that may additionally include dairy and/or eggs however have no meat, and vary in the amount of animal-based foods — Nata, such as semi-vegetarian diets that incorporate small amounts of meat. The Academy of Nutrition and Dietetics has released a role saying that well-planned plant diets help with health and are fantastic throughout life, inclusive for pregnancy, breastfeeding, childhood, adulthood, and athletes.

With earnings forecasting 60% growth by 2025, mostly a cause for concern for health, food security, and animal welfare, at some point in 2019 in the United States, the retail market for plant-based foods was once developing the familiar retail food market fee in eight instances.

Many sources use phrases such as plant-based weight loss plans to refer to diets such as different stages of animal products, defining "plant-based diets," for example, "diets" in which plants the beneficial amounts of ingredients and the number of animal foods are limited. "And as a diet" rich in vegetables and fruits, legumes, and minimally processed starchy staple content and limiting the consumption of purple meat if pink meat is eaten at all. " Others are" plant-based "and" Plant-only "distinguishes between. In

A range of sources, a" plant-based diet "has been used to:

Vegetarian: vegetables, legumes, fruits, grains, nuts, and seeds for weight loss plans, H However, no food from animal sources.

Fatalism: Vegetarian eating regimen specifically includes fruits.

Vegetarian: Vegetarian meal plan in which food is raw and dehydrated on occasion.

Vegetarianism: Vegetables, legumes, fruits, nuts, and grains weight loss Plans, in addition, may include eggs and dairy, but not meat.

Ovo-Lacto vegetarianism: includes dairy and eggs.

Ovo-vegetarian: contains eggs, but there is no dairy

Lacto vegetarian: it includes dairy, but no eggs.

Semi-Vegetarian: In the main vegetarian diet with the occasional inclusion of meat and/or poultry.

Macrobiotic diet: Semi-vegetarian weight loss plan that includes whole grains, vegetables, beans, miso soup, sea vegetables, and historically or naturally processed foods, including or with seafood and in addition to the different animal products.

Pescherian: Semi-vegetarian weight loss program with eggs, dairy, and seafood.

Flexitarian: Semi-vegetarian weight loss program, which includes limiting meat intake each day and/or being vegetarian only on certain days of the week.

Prehistoric Life

Although herbivores (reliance on the complete eating of plants) used to be a long-held concept to be a Mesozoic phenomenon, the evidence of this is fossilized as soon as it is determined that it should appear. Vegetated among terrestrial vertebrates with four limbs, tetrapods evolved into Late Carboniferous (307 - 299 million years ago). Early tetrapods were fish of large amphibians. While amphibians persevered to feed fishes and insects, some reptiles began to discover two new food types: tetrapod's (carnivorous) and plantains (herbivores).

Modern vegetarian and mild omnivores

often, usually, vegetarian creatures will consume small amounts of animal-based food when it becomes available. Although most trivial, omnivorous or herbivorous birds, such as sparrows, will regularly feed insects to their chickens, while food is expected to increase.

Similarly, monkeys of many species apparently eat maggots' fruits from time to time in want of sound fruit. When such animals are referred to as omnivores or otherwise, there is a question of context and emphasis as an alternative rather than a definition.

Human

Beings are omnivores, are able to use a variety of plant and animal foods. Fossil evidence from putts on enamel suggests the possibility that early homesteads such as strong Australopithecus and Homo habilis were opportunistic omnivores, usually present on a plant-based diet, although complementary to meat when possible.

A sustainable food diet can be measured through its phase of dietary adequacy, environmental sustainability, cultural acceptance, and affordability.

Input power refers to the processing, transport, storage, and service of food as opposed to the production of physical human energy. In contrast, environmental protection refers to the level of maintenance of ecosystems.

Plant-based diets can also contribute to reducing greenhouse gas emissions and the amount of land, water, and fertilizers used for agriculture. As a vast percentage of vegetation is used to feed livestock worldwide compared to humans, an increase in plant-based eating regimen may have additional contributions towards reducing climate change and loss of biodiversity. is. While "soy farming is the main driver of deforestation in the Amazon Basin," most soy plants are no longer destined for human consumption.

Subsequent blood pressure remained below 125/60 mmHg, HbA1c improved by 7.3%, and total cholesterol improved to 13 / mg / dL. Lisinopril was gradually reduced to 5 mg daily, and their diabetes is controlled with metformin at 1000 mg twice daily.

The case presented is a dramatic example of the impact on biometric outcomes such as blood pressure, diabetes, and lipid profile. A decrease in HbA1C from 11.1% to 6.3% in 3 months would be better than metformin or monotherapy with daily exercise.

Leading supporters in the field differ in opinions that include an optimal plant-based diet. Contrary to Ornis et all's a disease, animal products such as egg whites and skim milk allow small amounts.

A vegetarian or vegan diet adopted for moral or religious reasons may or may not be healthy. Thus, it is important to find out the details of a patient's diet, rather than knowing the specific definitions of the respective diets and making assumptions about how healthy it is. The following is a brief summary of specific diets that prohibit animal products. A major difference is that although most of these diets define what they exclude, plant-based diets are included.

Vegetarian (or total vegetarian): Exclude all animal products, especially meat, seafood, poultry, eggs, and dairy products.

Raw Food, Vegetarian: Same exclusion as well as the exclusion of all foods cooked at temperatures above 118 degrees Fahrenheit.

Lacto-vegetarian: Includes milk products except for eggs, meat, seafood, and poultry.

Ovo-vegetarian: Eggs, excluding meat, seafood, poultry, and dairy products.

Fish and olive oil are encouraged. Fat is not restricted.

Whole foods, plant-based, low-fat: encourage plant foods in their entire form, especially vegetables, fruits, legumes, and seeds and nuts (in small amounts). This diet limits animal products for maximum health benefits. Total fat is generally restricted.

Chapter 1: Advantages and Benefits of Plant-Based Diet

Obesity In 2006, after reviewing the facts from 87 published studies, authors Berko and Barnard 13 have noted in a nutritional review that a vegetarian or vegetarian diet is highly recommended for weight loss. He also said that the vegetarian population has low fees for coronary heart disease, excessive blood pressure, diabetes, and obesity. In addition, their assessment suggests that vegetarians are not established on a weight loss workout and are on a fee of about 1 pound per week. The authors further noted that a vegetarian weight loss plan brought on extra calories to be burned after a meal, in contrast to nonage diets, which may cause low energy burn as stored in fat.

Farmer et al. 14 states that a vegetarian diet may be better for weight management and more nutritious than a meat-eating diet. In their study, they confirmed that vegetarians were slimmer than their meat-eating counterparts. Vegetarians were prescribed to consume excess magnesium, potassium, iron, thiamine, riboflavin, folate and vitamins, and very little full fat. The authors conclude that vegetarian diets are nutrient-dense and may be recommended for weight management in addition to compromising the quality of the meal plan.

The findings also reported a large difference in age-adjusted BMI, with true BMI and vegetarian being lowest among meat-eaters. Similar results have been suggested through the Adventist Health Study.

According to Sabaté and Veen, "Epidemiological studies indicate that vegetarian diets are related to lower prevalence of BMI and obesity in adults and children. A meta-analysis of adult vegetarian dietary studies has estimated that for people 7.6 There has been a decrease in weight by 3.3 kg for kilograms and women, resulting in a lower 2-point BMI. Similarly, compared to nonvegetarians, vegetarian diets are leaner, and their BMI distinction increases during adolescence. Studies exploring opportunities for obesity and food agencies and dietary patterns suggest that a plant-based diet is a smart way to prevent weight problems in children. The strategy seems to be. Plant-based diets are low in power density and are high in complex carbohydrates, fiber, and water, which is additionally large as can be cultured and comfortable. "They need to be motivated to make health a plant-based diet pattern that concludes the author.

Diabetes

Plant-based diets may additionally provide benefits over these that are no longer plant-based with a thorough appreciation for the prevention and management of diabetes. Adventist Health Studies observed that vegetarians have almost half the risk of causing diabetes as non-scientific. A plant-based weight loss plan with little or no meat can help the forester and combat diabetes, with the help of increasing insulin sensitivity and reducing insulin resistance.

In 2006, Bernard et al. 21 stated that the results of a randomized clinical trial evaluated a low-fat vegetarian weight loss program based entirely on the guidelines of the American Diabetes Association. People on the low-fat vegetarian weight loss program lowered their HbA1c ranges using the 1.23 mark, as opposed to 0.38 points for humans on the American Diabetes Association diet. In addition, 43% of people on a low-fat vegetarian weight loss plan were able to limit their medication, compared to 26% on the diet of the American Diabetes Association.

In the Heart Disease

Lifestyle Heart Trial, Ornish 10, found that 82% of patients had a cardiovascular disease identified with some degree of regression of atherosclerosis with its application. Extensive lifestyle modifications show a catalyst delivering about this regression of extreme coronary atherosclerosis even after only 1 year. In their plant-based diet, 10% energy was constrained to fat, 15% to 20%

protein, and 70% to 75% from carbohydrates, and cholesterol once to 5 mg per day.

Interestingly, 53% of the management team had the development of atherosclerosis. After 5 years, the stenosis in the experimental group decreased from 37.8% to 34.7% (7.9% relative improvement). The manipulating team experienced the development of stenosis with 46.1% to 57.9% (27.7% relative worsening). Low-density lipoprotein had reduced 40% in 1 year and 20% less than baseline once 5 years. These markdowns are comparable to results performed with lipid-lowering drugs.

In the Lyon Diet Heart Study, De Lorgil, a prospective, randomized, secondary prevention trial, determined that the intervention team (at 27 months) experienced a 73% reduction in coronary events and a 70% reduction in all-cause mortality.

In 1998, a collaborative evaluation of the use of authentic facts from 5 prospective studies was reviewed and stated in the journal Public Health Nutrition. This is in contrast to the ischemic heart disease-specific mortality rate ratio of vegetarian and non-vegetarian people. Vegetarians had a 24% reduction in quotes from dying of ischemic coronary heart disease compared to non-vegetarians. Lower risk of ischemic coronary heart disease may be associated with lower cholesterol levels in humans who eat less meat.

Although vegetarian diets are associated with a decreased likelihood of many chronic diseases, different types of vegetarians may not ride the same results on health. The key is to focus on the intake of a healthy diet, not just a vegetarian or vegan diet.

The vegetarian diet is related to lower systolic blood stress and lowering of diastolic blood pressure. A randomized crossover trial determined that a Japanese diet (low sodium and plant-based) appreciably decreased systolic blood pressure.

Mortality

Guidelines Advisory Committee onDiet conducted a 2010 literature review to determine the effect of plant-based diets on stroke, heart disease, and mortality in adults. They found that plant-based diets are associated with a lower risk of cardiovascular disease and mortality than non-plant-based diets.

The benefit of a plant-based diet over mortality may be due to a decrease in the consumption of red meat in particular. Several types of research have documented the benefits of preventing excessive consumption of red meat, which is related to the risk of all-mortality and multiplication risk of heart mortality. 29 Reduced meat intakes are associated with longevity.

In 2012, Huang et al31 conducted a meta-analysis to observe heart disorder mortality among vegetarians and non-vegetarians. They only covered the research that stated the relative danger and the corresponding 95% confidence interval. Seven types of research were analyzed, with a total of 124,706 participants. Vegetarians had a 29% lower ischemic coronary heart disease mortality rate than no vegetarians.

Protein

Generally, patients are no longer at risk for protein deficiency in a plant-based weight loss program. Essential amino acids are observed in meat, dairy products, and eggs, such as many plant-based foods, such as quinoa.

Soybeans and ingredients made from soybeans are suitable sources of protein and may also help reduce blood density levels of low-density lipoproteins and reduce the risk of hip fracture 35 and some cancers.

Reduction in the vegetarian diet was related to systolic and diastolic blood stress ...

Iron

Plant-based diets include iron, although iron in the vegetation has lower bioavailability than meat. Plant-based ingredients that are rich in iron include kidney beans, black beans, soybeans, spinach, raisins, cashews, oatmeal, cabbage, and tomato juice. Iron shops may additionally be lower in those who follow a plant-based food regimen and eat little or no animal products. However, the American Dietetic Association states that iron deficiency anemia is uncommon even in humans who follow a diet in plants.

Vitamin B12

Individuals who follow a plant-based diet that does not contain any animal goods may be exposed to B12 deficient 40s and plan their meals with foods with vitamin B12, or nutritional B12 Want to complete.

Calcium and Vitamin D

Calcium consumption can be sufficient in a well-balanced, carefully planned, plant-based diet. People who no longer eat flowers that contain excessive amounts of calcium can also be at risk for impaired bone mineralization and fracture. Adequate calcium intake is the key to bone health, which seems likely regardless of dietary preferences. Some of the huge sources of calcium include tofu, mustard and turnip greens, book choy, and kale. Spinach and some isolated plant life contain calcium, although abundant, bound to oxalate and consequently poorly absorbed. It is advocated for those who are at risk for low bone mineral density and those who are located for vitamin D deficiency.

Using more fruits and vegetables, along with whole grains, lean meats, nuts, and beans, is a safe and healthy way to lose or maintain weight. In addition, diets rich in fruits and vegetables may reduce the risk of certain types of cancer and other persistent diseases. Fruits and vegetables also provide essential vitamins and minerals, fiber and other ingredients that are important for desirable health. To lose weight, you should consume less energy than your body uses. You can make low-calorie versions of some of your favorite dishes through the replacement of low-calorie fruits and vegetables in the vicinity of high-calorie content. Water and fiber will be added to your dishes in fruits and vegetables, so you can reduce the amount of low-calorie food. Most fruits and greens are naturally low in fat and calories and are filling.

A simple approach to reduce energy and eat extra fruits and greens at some point in the day.

Breakfast: Start the day with an egg or half of the cheese your morning omelet with spinach, onion, or mushroom. A dish with fewer calories than eggs or cheese will increase the amount and taste of veggies. Cut back on the amount of grain in your bowl to make room for some chopped bananas, peaches, or strawberries. You can still consume the entire bowl, but with fewer calories. Salads, tomatoes, cucumbers, or greens such as onions for 2 ounces and 2 ounces of onion. Meat, wrap, or burrito in your sandwich. The new version will fill you with fewer calories than the original.

In a broth-based soup, replace 2 ounces of meat or 1 cup of noodles with 1 cup of chopped vegetables such as broccoli, carrots, beans, or crimson peppers. Vegetables will help fill you up, so you won't give up these extra calories.

Add in 1 cup chopped greens such as broccoli, tomatoes, squash, onions or peppers, while casting 1 cup of rice or pasta in your favorite dish. The dish with vegetables will be just as satisfying, but the authentic version has fewer calories than the same amount. Take a precise look at your dinner plate. Vegetables, fruits, and whole grains are needed to take the largest element of your plate. If they don't, exchange some meat, cheese, white pasta, or rice with legumes, boiled broccoli, asparagus, greens, or any other favorite vegetable. This will reduce the overall energy in your food besides reducing the amount of food you eat. But note to use a normal or small size plate - there is no longer a plate. The full range of calories you count, even though a top percentage of them come from fruits and vegetables. Most nutritional consumption plans allow for one or two small snacks a day. Choosing most fruits and vegetables will allow you to eat a snack with only 100 calories. Instead of a high-calorie snack from a merchandising machine, take some cut-up greens or fruits from home. A 1-ounce bag of corn chips contains as many calories as a small apple, 1 cup whole strawberries, and 1 cup carrots as a 1/4 cup low-calorie dip. Substitute one or two of these options for chips, and you'll have an enjoyable snack with fewer calories. It is authentic that fruits and vegetables decrease in calories more than many different foods, but they contain few calories. If you start taking fruits and vegetables in addition to what you usually eat, you are adding energy and gaining weight as well. The key is a replacement. Eat fruits and vegetables instead of a few different high-calorie foods. Eat fruits and the way nature has provided, or with fat-free or low-fat cooking techniques.

Try steaming your vegetables, use a low-calorie or low-fat dressing, and use herbs and spices to add flavor. Some cooking techniques, such as braiding and frying, or the use of high-fat dressings or sauces, will increase the calories and fat content in the dish. And eat unripe fruits to revel in your herbal sweetness.

Canned or frozen fruits and vegetables are also the perfect choices.

Frozen or canned fruits and greens can be just as nutritious as clean varieties. However, be cautious to exclude these without introducing sugar, syrup, cream sauce, or various ingredients that add calories.

Choose total fruit over fruit drinks and juices. Fruit juice has led to a shortage of fiber in fruits.

It is better to eat whole fruit because it contains added fiber, which helps you to feel full. A 6-ounce medium orange of orange juice contains eighty-five calories as opposed to just sixty-five calories. Whole fruit provides you with a larger measurement snack for similar fruits with more calories than dried fruits.

A small container (1/4 cup) of raisins is about one hundred calories. For the same range of calories, you can eat 1 cup of grapes.

Seitan

Seitan is a well-known protein source for many vegetarian and vegetarian people. It is made from gluten, which is the main protein in wheat. Unlike many soy-based mock types of meat, it resembles the texture of meat when cooked. Also known as wheat meat or wheat gluten, it incorporates 3.5 grams per 25 grams of protein. (100 grams). It supplies the richest plant protein in this list. Satan is also a perfect supply of selenium and contains small amounts of iron, calcium, and phosphorus.

You can alternatively find this meat in the refrigerated portion of most health food stores, or make your own version with significant wheat gluten using this recipe. Cetaphil can be fried, fried, and even grilled. Therefore, it can be easily integrated into a range of dishes. However, celiac should be prevented with the help of people with celiac disease or gluten sensitivity.

Tofu, and Adame

Temehtofu, Tempe, and Edamame all originate from soybeans. Soybeans are seen as a complete supply of protein. It is this ability that supplies the physique with all the essential amino acids. Adame is immature soybeans with candy and slightly grassy flavor. They need to be boiled or steamed before consumption and can be eaten on their own or served with soups and salads. Tofu is made from bean curd that is pressed together in a system similar to a cheesecake. The tempeh is made from ripe soybeans before cooking and a little fermentation so that they can be placed in a patty. Tofu does not contain tons of flavor, although it easily absorbs the flavor of the components with which it is formulated. In comparison, tempeh has a characteristic nutritious flavor.

Both tofu and tempeh can be used in a range of dishes, ranging from burgers to soups and chilies. All three contain iron, calcium, and 10–19 grams of protein per 3.5 ounces. (100 grams).

Edamame is additionally rich in folate, vitamin K and fiber. Tempeh contains an excellent number of probiotics, B nutritional vitamins, and minerals such as magnesium and phosphorus. Lentil. At 18 grams of protein per cooked cup (240 ml), dal is an exceptional supply of protein.

They can be used in a variety of dishes, from clean salads to hearty soups and spices to drench dahls. Lentils also contain the top amount of slowly digested carbs, and a cup (240 ml) advocates for about 50% of your day-long fiber intake. In addition, the type of fiber found in lentils has been proven to feed desirable bacteria into your colon, which supplies a healthy gut. Lentils may additionally help reduce the risk of heart disease, diabetes, excess body weight, and certain types of cancer. In addition, lentils are rich in folate, manganese and iron. In addition, they contain a fair number of antioxidants and various health-promoting plant compounds.

Beans Chickpeas and most varieties of

kidney, kale, pinto, and most different types of beans contain high amounts of protein per serving. Chickpeas, also accepted as Garbanzo beans, are some other legumes with high protein content. Both beans and chickpeas contain about 15 grams of protein per cooked cup (240 ml). They are additionally terrific sources of complex carbs, fiber, iron, folate, phosphorus, potassium, manganese and various recommended plant compounds. In addition, many types of research suggest that weight loss plans in beans and other beans can lower cholesterol, control blood sugar levels, lower blood pressure, and even reduce belly fat Helps.

Nutritional yeast

Nutritional yeast is a dedicated strain of Saccharomyces cerevisiae yeast, which is given commercially in the form of yellow powder or flax. It has a delicious taste, making it a well-known ingredient in dishes such as mashed potatoes and fried tofu. Nutritious yeast can also be sprinkled on the crest of pasta dishes or even enjoyed as savory toppings on popcorn. This complete source of plant protein provides a physique with 14 grams of protein and 7 grams of fiber per ounce (28 grams). There is a beautiful supply of fortified nutritional yeast, B12, as well as zinc, magnesium, copper, manganese, and all B vitamins. However, fortifications are no longer accepted and should not rely on the unfortunate dietary yeast as a source of diet B12.

Sponsored and Teff

belong to a category recognized as historical cereals. Other historical cereals include anchorage, barley, sorghum, and farro. Spawning is a type of wheat and contains gluten, while teff originates from an annual grass, which is potentially gluten-free.

Spilled and teff provides 10–12 grams of protein per cooked cup (240 ml) compared to individual historical grains, making them high in protein. Both are outstanding sources of more than a few nutrients consisting of complex nutrients, fiber, iron, magnesium, phosphorus, and manganese. In addition, they contain the right amount of B vitamins, zinc and selenium. Sponsored and teff is versatile options for mango grains, such as wheat and rice, and can be used in many dishes, from baked items to polenta and risotto.

Hempseed

hemp seed comes from the cannabis Sativa plant, which is notorious for belonging to the same house as the marijuana plant. But hempseed only indicates the amount of THC, the compound that produces drug effects such as marijuana.

Although no longer as prevalent as other seeds, hemp seed contains 10 grams of full, digestible protein per ounce (28%) without difficulty. It is 50% more than chia seeds and flaxseed. Hemp seeds also contain appropriate amounts of magnesium, iron, calcium, zinc, and selenium. What's more, it is an appropriate source of omega-3 and omega-6 fatty acids that are most efficient for human health. Interestingly, some research suggests that the types of fat found in hemp seeds may additionally limit inflammation, as well as reduce symptoms of PMS, menopause, and some skin diseases.

Green peas A

Little inexperienced peas are often served as a side dish that contains 9 grams of protein per cooked cup (240 ml), barely extra than a cup of milk. What's more, a serving of inexperienced peas covers more than 25% of your everyday fiber, diet A, C, K, thiamine, folate, and manganese requirements. Green peas are also a suitable supply of iron, magnesium, phosphorus, zinc, copper, and countless other B vitamins. You can use the peas in dishes such as peas and basil stuffed ravioli, Thai-inspired pea soup or peas and avocado guacamole.

Spirulina

This blue-green alga is definitely a dietary center. Two tablespoons (30 ml) provide you with 22% iron and thiamine and 42% of your daily copper needs, plus eight grams of whole protein, in addition to meeting your day-to-day copper needs. Spirulina additionally contains a respectable amount of magnesium, riboflavin, manganese, potassium, and low amounts of various vitamins of your body as well as essential fatty acids. The natural pigment phycocyanin prescribed in Spicolina has powerful antioxidant, anti-inflammatory and anti-cancer properties. In addition, research hyperlinks consume Spirulina for health benefits from more beneficial immune tools and reduce blood stress in elevated blood sugar and LDL cholesterol levels.

Amaranth and Quinoa are

Although routinely referred to as historical or gluten-free grains, Amaranth and Quinoa are not developed from grasses like other cereal grains. For this reason, they are technically considered to be "pseudo-collectives."

Nevertheless, they can be prepared or floored in flour equivalent to grains considered more regularly. In addition, amaranth and quinoa are suitable sources of complex carbs, fiber, iron, manganese, phosphorus, and magnesium: Ezekiel bread and other bread made from sprouted grains. Ezekiel bread is made from organic, sprouted whole grains and beans. They contain wheat, millet, barley, and spices, as well as soybeans and lentils.

Two slices of Ezekiel bread contain about 8 grams of protein, a little extra than a mango bread. Sprouted grains and legumes increase the number of nutritious nutrients and decrease the number of anti-nutrients in them.

In addition, studies show that sprouts increase their amino acid content. Lysine limits amino acids in many plants and sprouting increases the amount of lysine. This helps promote normal protein quality. Similarly, combining grains with legumes is needed to improve the amino acid profile of bread further.

Sprouting also increases the amount of soluble fiber, folate, diet C, vitamin E and beta-carotene of bread. It can also reduce the gluten content slightly, which can beautify digestion in these sensitive to gluten.

Soy Milk

Milk It is made from soybean and is an excellent alternative to fortified cow's milk with nutritional vitamins and minerals. On the whole, it does not contain 7 grams of protein per cup (240 ml), although it is a very good supply of calcium, diet D, and nutrition B12. However, keep in mind that soy milk and soybeans no longer naturally contain nutritional B12, so it is recommended to select a firm category. Soy milk is prescribed in most supermarkets. It is a very versatile product that can be eaten on its own or in a variety of cooking and baking dishes. It is an accurate idea to choose unirrigated varieties to keep the amount of distributed sugars to a minimum.

Oats and Oatmeal

Oats are a convenient and great way to add protein to any diet. Half a cup (120 ml) dry oats provide you with about 6 grams of protein and four grams of fiber. This part contains the top amount of magnesium, zinc, phosphorus, and folate. Although oats are no longer viewed as whole proteins, they contain high-quality proteins, which normally consume various grains such as rice and wheat. You can use oats in a variety of recipes ranging from oatmeal to veggie burgers. They can additionally be floored in flour and can be used for baking.

Wild Rice Wild Rice

It Contains about 1.5 instances, as do other long-grain rice varieties that contain a lot of protein, including brown rice and basmati. A cooked cup (240 ml) provides 7 grams of protein, in addition to fiber, manganese, magnesium, copper, phosphorus, and a correct amount of B vitamins. Unlike white rice, wild rice does not snatch its bran. This is top-notch from a dietary point of view because bran contains abundant amounts of fiber and vitamins and minerals.

However, these purposes concern arsenic, which may accumulate in the bran of rice plants grown in polluted areas. Arsenic is a toxic trace factor that can also exacerbate many types of health problems, especially when ingested in many cases over a long period of time. Washing wild rice before cooking and using lots of water to boil can also limit the amount of arsenic to 57%.

Chia Seeds

Chia seeds are obtained from the Salvia plant, which is native to Mexico and Guatemala. At 6 grams of protein and thirteen grams of fiber per 1.25 ounces (35 grams), chia seeds absolutely deserve their place on this list.

What's more, these small seeds contain the right amounts of iron, calcium, selenium, and magnesium, as well as more than omega-3 fatty acids, antioxidants, and some other beneficial plant compounds. They are also particularly versatile. Chia seeds have a bland style and are capable of being converted into a gel-like substance in water. This makes them an easy addition to a range of dishes, from smoothies to baked items and chia pudding.

Fatty Acids are essential fatty acids that humans must ingest for precise fitness because our bodies no longer synthesize them. Only two such important fatty acids are known: linoleic acid (one omega-6 fatty acid) and alpha-linolenic acid (one omega-3 fatty acid).

A plant-based diet is not an all-and-nothing program, but a way of life that suits every individual. It can be especially beneficial for obese people, type 2 diabetes, hypertension, lipid disorders, or heart disease. Obesity and diabetes patients will benefit from a plant-based diet that includes moderate amounts of fruits and vegetables and low-fat animal products. Severe obesity may require low-calorie diets or very-low-calorie diets and consultation and initial management with the supervision of a physician's team. Kidney disease patients may require a plant-based diet with special restrictions, for example, fruits and vegetables that are high in potassium and phosphorus.

Practitioners should advocate that it should be able to get away from terms like vegetarian and vegan and to eat healthy, whole, plant-based foods (mainly fruits and vegetables) and reduce consumption of meat, eggs and dairy products. I have to talk about it.

Very often, physicians ignore the potential benefits of good nutrition and prescribe medicines quickly rather than giving patients the chance to cure their illness through healthy eating and staying active.

If we are to reduce the obesity epidemic and reduce the complications of chronic disease, then we should consider changing the mind-set of our culture from "eat to live" to "eat to live." The future of health care will include evolution.

Chapter 2: Example of A Balanced Meal Plan and Useful Tips That Will Help You Every Day

Nevertheless, the fitness and wellbeing community agrees that the diet emphasizes fresh, whole foods, and minimizing processed food is the most effective for standard wellness.

Whole foods, plant-based weight loss plans do just that.

It focuses on minimally processed foods, especially plants, and is fantastic at reducing weight and improving health.

There is no clear definition of what constitutes a complete food, plant-based weight loss plan (WFPB diet). The WFPB meal plan is no longer always a defined meal plan - this is in addition to the lifestyle.

Nevertheless, the primary concepts of whole foods, plant-based food diet are as follows:

Emphasizes whole, minimally processed foods e limits or avoids animal products

The focus is on plants, which include vegetables, fruits, whole grains, legumes, seeds, and nuts, which make up the majority of what they eat.

Refined foods are included, such as sugar, white flour, and processed oil.

Paying special attention to the quality of the food, the WFPB sells sourced, organic food domestically on every occasion with many supporters of food.

For these reasons, this weight loss plan often accompanies a vegetarian or vegan diet. Still similar in some ways, but now these diets are not the same.

People who follow a vegetarian diet by eating any animal products, along with dairy diet, meat, poultry, seafood, eggs, and honey. Vegetarians eliminate all meat and cock from their diet, but some vegetarians eat eggs, seafood, or dairy.

On the other hand, the WFPB diet is extra flexible. Followers consume on whole plants, although animal traders are not far from the border.

Obesity is a difficulty in epidemic proportions. In fact, more than 69% of US adults are overweight or obese.

Fortunately, changing diet and ways of life can facilitate weight loss and have lasting effects on health.

An assessment of 12 research involving more than 1,100 humans found that over 18 weeks were assigned to plant-based diets that weighed significantly - about 4.5 kg (2 kg) - assigned to non-vegetarian diets. I went.

Adopting healthy plant-based eating samples can additionally help maintain weight for a longer period of time.

Sixty-five overweight and obese adults received information about who was assigned to these WFBB diets who lost excess weight compared to the control team and weighed 9.25 kg (4.2 kg) at a one-year follow-up Were able to subtract.

In addition, obviously reducing processed foods that are not allowed on WFPB food diets like soda, candy, quick meals, and refined grains is an effective weight-loss tool.

Adopting a whole-food, plant-based diet not only benefits your waistline, but it can also reduce your risk and reduce the signs and symptoms of some chronic diseases.

Heart Disease

It is probably one of the most customary benefits of the WFPB diet is that they are heart-healthy.

However, the quality and type of material involved in the case of a weight loss plan.

A large study in more than 200,000 humans stated that people who are rich in vegetables, fruits, whole grains, legumes, and nuts with a healthy plant-based diet, compared to their non-plant-based coronary heart disease the risk of developing diet has decreased significantly.

However, unhealthy plant-based diets that protected sugary drinks, fruit juices, and micro-grains were associated with a barely increased likelihood of coronary heart disease.

Eating the right type of food is important for the prevention of heart disease when following a plant-based diet, which is why following the WFPB food plan is a great option.

Cancer

Research suggests that following a plant-based weight loss program can reduce your risk of positive types of cancer.

Pescatarian (fish-consuming vegetarians) had the greatest protection from colorectal cancer, reducing it by 43% compared to carnivores.

Cognitive Deterioration

Plant-based diets contain a large range of plant compounds and antioxidants, which have been proven to develop Alzheimer's disorder and reverse cognitive deficits progressively.

In several studies, a high intake of fruits and greens has been strongly associated with a decrease in cognitive decline.

An evaluation of nine types of research, such as over 31,000 humans, showed that consuming more fruits and vegetables reduced the risk of cognitive impairment or dementia by 20%.

Diabetes

Adopting the WFPB diet plan can also be a tremendous tool in managing and reducing your chance of developing diabetes.

A study in more than 200,000 humans stated that those who followed a nutritious plant-based eating sample had a 34% lower risk of developing diabetes with an unhealthy, non-plant-based diet.

Adopting whole foods, plant-based diets are good for the planet.

Switching to a plant-based diet plan now not only benefits your health - it can help protect the environment, as well.

Those who follow a plant-based diet have a tendency to have small environmental footprints.

Adoption of sustainable eating habits can aid greenhouse fuel emissions, water consumption, and land used for manufacturing unit farming, which are all elements of global warming and environmental degradation.

An evaluation of thirty-three researches showed that the greatest environmental benefits were seen from diets with the least amount of animal-based diets, such as vegan, vegetarian, and Pasteurian diets.

It was stated that 50% to meet the 70% discount in greenhouse gasoline emissions and land use and the Western weight loss program pattern as a more sustainable, plant-based dietary pattern. Very little water should be used.

What's more, reducing the number of animal traders in their weight loss plans and buying local, sustainable produce boosts the local financial system and reduces reliance on manufacturing facility farming, a sustainable approach to food production.

From eggs and bacon to breakfast to dinner, animal wares are the focus of food for many.

A Full-Food, Plant-Based Shopping List

Fruits: berries, citrus fruits, pears, peaches, pineapples

Whole Grains: Brown Rice, Rolled Oats, Parsley, Quinoa, Brown Rice Pasta, Barley, etc.

Nuts and nut butter: almonds, cashews, macadamia nuts, pumpkin seeds, sunflower seeds, herbal peanut butter, tahini, etc.

Unfermented plant-based milk: coconut Milk, Almonds. Milk, Cashew Milk, etc.

Spices, Herbs, and Spices.: Basil, rosemary, turmeric, curry, black pepper, salt, etc.

Spices: Salsa, mustard, diet yeast, soy sauce, vinegar, lemon juice, etc.

Plant-based protein: Tofu, Tempeh, plant-based protein source or powder without sugar or artificial ingredients.

Beverages: Coffee, tea, sparkling water, etc.

If you supplement a plant-based weight loss program with animal products, choose great products from grocery stores or, better yet, buy them from local farms.

Eggs: Pasture-raised when possible.

Poultry: Free-range, natural when possible.

Beef and Pork: Pasta or hay is fed when possible.

Seafood: The wild is caught from permanent fishes when possible.

Dairy: Organic dairy products from pastured animals possible every time.

The WFPB weight loss plan is a method of eating that focuses on eating foods in their most natural form. This skill excludes heavily processed materials.

When shopping for groceries, focus on fresh food and, when buying food with a label, aim for the items with the lowest possible ingredients.

Fast foods: French fries, cheeseburgers, hot dogs, poultry nuggets, etc.

Processed Vegan-friendly food: Plant-based meats like Tofurkey, Fox Cheese, Veg Butter, etc.

Artificial. Sweeteners: Equal, Splenda, Sweets' Less, etc.

Processed Animal Products: Bacon, Lunch Meats, Sausage, Pork Jerky, etc.,

To minimize foods while healthy animal ingredients can be blanketed into the WFPB diet Is, the following products should be. The least of all plant-based diets.

Beef

Pork

Sheep

Game Meat

Poultry

Eggs

Dairy

Seafood

Transition to whole foods, plant-based weight loss plans need not be challenged.

Example 1: A Week Plant-Based Diet Meal Plan

The following one-week menu can help set you up for success. There are many types of animal products involved; however, the extent to which you are involved with animal foods in your weight loss plan is up to you.

MONDAY

Breakfast: Oatmeal with coconut milk.

Lunch: Large salads topped with sparkling vegetables, chickpeas, avocados, pumpkin seeds, and goat cheese.

Dinner: Butternut Squash Curry.

TUESDAY

Breakfast: Full-fat waterless yogurt, sliced strawberries, uncooked coconut, and pumpkin seeds.

Lunch: Meatless Chili.

Dinner: sweet potato and black bean tacos.

WEDNESDAY

Breakfast: A smoothie made of unripe coconut milk, berries, peanut butter, and unleavened plant-based protein powder.

Lunch: hummus and veggie wrap.

Dinner: Zucchini noodles tossed in pesto with fowl meatballs.

THURSDAY

Breakfast: Serve porridge with avocado, salsa, and black beans.

Lunch: Quinoa, Veggie, and Feta Salad.

Dinner: grilled fish with roasted candy potatoes and broccoli.

FRIDAY

Breakfast: Vegetable Frittata.

Lunch: grilled shrimp.

Dinner: Portobello Fajitas.

SATURDAY

Breakfast: Blackberry, Kale

Lunch: Brown rice sushi with a seaweed salad.

Dinner: Brinjal lasagna with cheese and a giant green salad.

SUNDAY

Breakfast: Made with Vegetable Omelets Eggs.

Lunch: Roasted vegetables and tahini quinoa bowl.

Dinner: The black bean burger is served on a huge salad with sliced avocado.

As you can see, the concept of a whole-food, plant-based food plan is to use the animal trade sparingly.

However, many humans who follow WFPB diets eat more or less animal products dependent on their specific diets and preferences.

Example 2: 4-Week Plant-Based Diet Meal Plan

Week 1

Pick at least three dinners to prepare dinner at home and reproduction them into your Healthy Meal Plan spreadsheet on the days for Week 1! On days you're now not cooking, use up leftovers or do "clean out the fridge" meals, and allow for foods out.

- Mediterranean Veggie Sandwich
- Best Teriyaki Vegetable Stir Fry
- Chickpea Couscous Bowls with Tahini Sauce
- Chipotle Black Bean Tortilla Soup

Week 2

Pick at least 3 dinners to prepare dinner at home and copy them into your Healthy Meal Plan spreadsheet on the days for Week 2! On days you're no longer cooking, use up leftovers or do "clean out the fridge" meals, and enable for foods out.

- Weeknight Chickpea Curry

- Mexican Sweet Potatoes
- Cauliflower Tacos with Yum Yum Sauce
- Make again! 1 or 2 favored dinner thoughts from Week 1

Week 3

Pick at least 3 dinners to cook at home and copy them into your Healthy Meal Plan spreadsheet on the days for Week 3! On days you're no longer cooking, use up leftovers or do "clean out the fridge" meals, and permit for ingredients out.

- Greek Nachos with Cilantro Drizzle
- Quick Cuban Black Beans
- Tomato Coconut Cauliflower Curry
- Make again! 1 or 2 favorite dinner thoughts from Week 1 of 2

Week 4

Pick at least three dinners to cook at domestic and copy them into your Healthy Meal Plan spreadsheet on the days for Week 4! On days you're now not cooking, use up leftovers or do "clean out the fridge" meals, and enable for meals out.

- BBQ Bean Tacos with Pineapple Salsa
- Tuscan Soup with White Beans
- Jackfruit BBQ Sandwich
- Make again! 1 or 2 preferred dinner thoughts from Week 1, 2 or 3

Chapter 3: Plant-Based Breakfast Recipes

Black Forest Overnight Oats

Ingredients

- Porridge
- 55g| Be sure to buy ½ cup rolled oats if necessary, gluten-free oats.

- 1 Tbsp Cocoa Powder
- 1 Tbsp Chia Seeds
- 1 Tbsp Chocolate Chips (I use Camino Chocolate Chips because they are organic, fair-trade; however, there are roughly other vegetarian types on hand as Vezina).
- 1/2 teaspoon vanilla extract
- 1 tbsp maple syrup
- 185mls | ¾ cup non-dairy milk
- 110g | Half a cup half a cherry (extracted stones - can use frozen and defrosted cherries) for
- chocolate sauce (optional)
- 1 tbsp chocolate chips
- 1 tablespoon non-dairy milk

Instructions

- All ingredients of oatmeal without a cherry in a lidded jar or add to separate sealable containers (I use a 16oz largemouth mason jar).
- Stir properly or put the lid on and stir to mix completely.
- Top the oatmeal with cherries, keep the lid in the fridge for at least eight hours and keep coconut cream for coconut cream
- Before serving.
- Add a can of full-fat coconut milk for at least 24 hours.

- Open the can and spread the challenging part into the bowl. Place the liquid phase for a smoothie or add to the curry.
- Whip with an electrically operated hand mixer or let the mixer stand until light and fluffy. Might make enough cream for at least a couple of oatmeal jars depending on how generous you are with it.

Chocolate Sauce

- Chocolate and the chips to a small bowl or pan with milk and heat very gently until melted. I used a microwave, and it actually took about 10 seconds. Stir collectively until smooth.
- Remove oatmeal from the fridge, spoon on some whipped coconut cream, and drizzle with chocolate sauce. Top with a cherry or two!

Sun-Dried Chicken Pancakes with Tomato Sauce

Ingredients

- 1 cup chickpea flour
- 1 cup of water
- 1 teaspoon baking powder
- 1 tbsp basil or oregano
- 1 teaspoon olive oil (optional)

- salt, pepper, chili
- sun tomato sauce
- dried 5 Tomatoes
- 10 Cherry Tomatoes
- Garlic 1
- Sparkling Basil Kutti

Instructions

- a small bowl mixes together the flour, water, baking powder, and spices. As long as no flakes remain.
- In a small pan, use a nonstick wok or hot olive oil and add the mixture and spread it out. Cook both strands for 5 minutes or until they are no longer sticky.
- While pancakes are adding tomatoes, sun-dried tomatoes, basil, and garlic to the cooking processor and mix until smooth. Serve pancake hot with tomato sauce and toppings of your choice! As a pleasure!

Snickerdoodle Energetics

Ingredients

- 1 cup sweet large rock coconut, 2 ounces
- 2 cups almonds, 9 ounces
- 2 cups pecans, 8 ounces
- 1 tablespoon Vietnamese
- cinnamon 12 Medjool dates pitted and quartered
- 1vanilla extract
- teaspoon 1/2 teaspoon sea salt
- 2 teaspoon maple syrup
- 1-2 Tablespoon Water Place

Instructions

- Add vanilla, sea salt, and maple syrup. The process once until combined, about 20 seconds.

- Taste the combination and see if it is sweet enough, if not you can add a little extra maple syrup to the water area. You can add extra cinnamon if you want.

- 1/2. Makes it thicker. This will take up about 3/4 of the pan. Using a chef's knife reduces this to 30 times.

- From here, you can wrap the two individually or spread them on a pair of cookie sheets before putting them together in a container and placing them in the freezer again. These bars last 4-5 days in the refrigerator and 1 month in the freezer.

Chocolate Chips with Strawberry Banana Baked Oatmeal Cutting

Ingredients

- 2 Bananas (smashed) (about 1 cup)
- 1 cup non-dairy milk (I used WestSoy organic image available)
- 1 teaspoon vanilla extract
- 3 cups customary antique oats (use to make certified gluten-free Jiyh recipe gluten-free)
- 2 tablespoons flax meal
- 1½ teaspoons baking powder
- 1/4 teaspoon salt

- 1 teaspoon cinnamon
- 2 cups cleaned strawberries (chopped)
- 1/4 cup non-dairy chocolate chips (Vakil Pic)

Instructions

- Preheat oven to 350 grams f.
- A muffin pan with light spray oil (I used coconut oil).
- In a medium bowl, combine the mashed banana, milk, and vanilla together.
- In another bowl, combine oats, flax, baking powder, salt, and cinnamon.
- Pour dry ingredients in moist and stir until well combined.
- Stir in strawberries and chocolate chips (if using).
- Fill the muffin tins with the oatmeal mixture and press them gently to compact them.
- Bake for 20-25 minutes until the edges are golden brown and the oatmeal is baked through.
- Let cool in the pan on a wire rack for at least 10 minutes. This will ensure that oatmeal bites are organized and preserved simultaneously.
- Take the oatmeal out of the muffin pan and enjoy it!
- Store any leftovers in the fridge.

Fluffy Vegetarian Pancake

Ingredients

- 1/2 cup (120 g) apple
- 1/2 cup (120 g) non-dairy milk
- 1 tbsp lemon juice
- unripe 1-2 tablespoons maple syrup (optional)
- 1 tablespoon vanilla extract
- 1 1/4 cup (150 grams) grits
- 1/2 teaspoon baking powder

- 1/2 tsp baking soda
- 1/4 tsp salt

Instructions

- Whisk together apples, non-dairy milk, maple syrup, lemon juice, and vanilla.
- Add dry ingredients. Stir to combine (do not overdo the mixture until all the lumps are gone).
- Heat a pan on low heat.
- Put about 1/4 cup of batter in the preheated pan.
- Cook for 4-5 minutes or until the edges are brown. Flip over — Cook every 4-5 minutes. Take your time, slow and slow, honestly here is the secret.
- Repeat until all the batter is long (I usually get 6 pancakes per batch)
- Top with fruits enjoys maple syrup, chocolate chips, etc.!

Breakfast Tacos

Ingredients

- 1/2 onion,
- one 1/2 pepper,
- one 1/2 jalapeno (remove seeds for very low heat),
- 1 handful of mushrooms, chopped
- 1 cup cabbage
- 1 mass cooked potato,

- 1 / 2 for 1 cup of cooked beans, dry
- 1/2 cup cooked quinoa
- 1 nourishing yeast
- salt (or black salt), black pepper, garlic, turmeric and alternative to flavored
- gluten-free tortillas of your choice, use corn tortillas

Instructions

- Add onion, Boiling peppers and mushrooms and prepare dinner over medium heat, sometimes shaking, and start wedges sticking that little shaking water.
- Once the stir in potatoes, quinoa and beans begin to soften. They will start clinging now.
- As soon as the entirety is included and, in the summer, add nutritional yeast and spices.
- Drain it in tortillas and serve.

Every Quinoa Breakfast Bowl

Ingredients

- 1 cup Raw Quinoa
- 2 cups (470 ml) Almond Milk
- 1 Tablespoon Maple Syrup
- Fresh Fruits: Strawberries, Raspberries, Blueberries, Blueberries,
- Butter for, Alternative
- Kaka Nib, Optional

Instructions

SprinklingCook of Quinoa According to Cucino. Just use almond milk instead of water.

Wash your favorite fruits. Mix in a bowl collectively with the cooked quinoa. Sprinkle with nut butter and optionally available cacao nib.

Blueberry Swirl Buckwheat, Amaranth Shells

Ingredients

- 1/3 cup buckwheat
- 1/3 cup amaranth
- 1 cup raw walnuts
- 1 Tbs. Apple cider vinegar or lemon juice
- 4 cups blueberries, sparkling or frozen
- 1 Tbs. Raw honey or maple syrup

- 1/2 tsp. Cardamom
- 1/4 tsp. Cinnamon
- water sea salt
- 1/2 tsp. Pure vanilla extracts
- 1 / 2- 1 1/2 cups water, split

Instructions:

Walnuts, amaranth, and buckwheat cover with warm water and lemon juice or a spoonful of apple cider vinegar. Allow soaking overnight. The next morning, drain and rinse well.

In a food processor or blender, puree the blueberries and honey until they are smooth. Spoon out about half a puree and set aside.

Add to the dry and rinsed nuts and seeds, with spices and with about half a cup of water, without removing the final puree. Blend puree until smooth.

To assemble and eat, spoon into a small saucepan with enough water in a thin saucepan if necessary. This will depend on your berries. Heat until it forms a thick porridge. Then, roll a few tablespoons of blueberry puree into each portion. Top with more blueberries and walnuts, if desired.

Vegetarian German Chocolate Pancakes

Pancake:

- 1 1/2 cups gluten-free all-cause flour
- 1/4 cup cocoa powder
- unsweetened2 tsp baking powder
- 1/2 cup mashed banana or apple
- 1 1/4 cup Thai Kitchen Mild Coconut Milk
- 2 tsp pure vanilla extract

- 1/4 sea salt
- 3 maple syrup

Topping:

- Tispunteblspun 3/4 cup smooth Pud Medjul palm (if they are soft not, then soak them in filtered water for 30 minutes before using in recipes Dry well Chci)
- 3 tablespoons pecan butter (or almond butter)
- 1 teaspoon pure vanilla extract
- Pinch sea salt
- 1/3 cup filtered water, or as needed
- 1/3 cup finely shredded coconut
- 1 / 4 cups chopped walnuts
- Mini Veg Chocolate Chips (optional)

Pumpkin Seeds and Chocolate Chip Oatmeal Breakfast Bar

Ingredients

- 11/2 cups rolled oats
- 11/4 cups oat flour table
- 3–4spoon pumpkin seeds
- 2-3 large Cham in neither permissible Ri chocolate chips or mini chips (raisins or dried cranberries can be changed)

- 1 teaspoon cinnamon
- 1/4 teaspoon sea salt
- 1 / 8-1 / 4 teaspoon fresh peas add nutmeg
- 1/4 cup plus 2 tablespoons non-dairy milk
- 1/3 cup brown rice syrup
- 1-2 tablespoons pure maple syrup

Instructions

- Unbaked preheat oven to 350 ° F. Line an 8 a × 8 ″ baking dish with parchment paper. In a large bowl, mix oat flour, grits, pumpkin seeds, chocolate chips, cinnamon, sea salt, and nutmeg.
- In a small bowl, combine milk, brown rice syrup and maple syrup.
- Add moist ingredients to the dry mixture, stirring until properly combined.

Carrot and Coconut Breakfast Bowl

Ingredients

- 3 teaspoons chia seeds
- 4 teaspoons oats
- 1 cup of coconut milk cup
- ½carrot juice
- 1 teaspoon cinnamon
- 1 banana
- 1 teaspoon peanut butter
- maple syrup (optional)

Instructions

- milk and carrots, place cinnamon chia. The seeds and oats juice in a bowl and stir them well together. Cover the bowl and store it in the fridge overnight or for at least a few hours.

- Once the combination is soft, take it out of the fridge. Add peanut butter and sliced bananas. You can sweeten it if needed. Mix well together! As a pleasure!

Turmeric Steel Cut Oats Recipe

Ingredients

- 1/4 tsp (0.25 tsp) oil
- 1/2 cup (2.82 oz) metal-reducing oats use certified gluten-free if needed.
- 1 ½ cup (13.23 oz) water2 cups thinner consistency

- 1 cup (8.61) oz) non-dairy milk
- 1/3 tsp (0.33 tsp) or more turmeric
- 1 / 3-1 / 2 tsp (0.33 tsp) cinnamon
- 1/4 tsp (0.25 tsp) or more cardamom
- 1 / 8 tsp (0.13 tsp) salt sweets of
- 2 tbsp or more maple or various choice Male.

Instructions

- Heat oil in a saucepan on medium heat. Add oats and toast for 2 minutes or until fragrant.
- Add water and milk and mix. bring to a boil. (About 5 minutes)
- Reduce heat to medium-low. Stir and proceed to cook for 10 minutes.
- Mix in spices, salt, and maple and cook dinner for another 7 minutes or longer until the oats are cooked to preference. Modify and modify the candy and flavor. Oats will be a few minutes longer if you double/increase the recipe.
- There will probably be some more liquid in the saucepan. The liquid is absorbed through the oats as the oatmeal sits. Cook for a few minutes or let it cool for 10-15 minutes.
- Garnish with chopped strawberries, chia seeds, papaya seeds, currents, or different clean or dried fruits of choice. Serve hot or cold.

Breakfast Chia Kheer

Ingredients

- 1 Medjool Date, Pit Removed
- 1 Cup Non-Dairy Milk, Natural Soya, Almond or Coconut
- 1 Fist Sparkling Spinach
- 3 Karachi Chia Seeds
- Topping (Optional), Banana, Kiwi, Mango, Berries, etc. For Fruits

Instructions

- Fast Speed In the blender, combine the dates, milk, and spinach.
- In a medium bowl, add liquid to the chia seeds.
- Stir well, and continue stirring every few minutes for about 15 minutes.
- Keep in the fridge for at least an hour or overnight.
- Stir again before serving, then peak with fruit.

Flour Omelet

Ingredients

- 1/4 cup Chikoos flour
- 1 TB nutritional yeast
- 1/2 teaspoon baking powder
- 1/4 teaspoon turmeric

- 1/2 teaspoon chopped CIWS or 1/4 teaspoon onion powder
- 1/4 teaspoon garlic powder
- 1 / 8 TSP Black Pepper
- 1/2 teaspoon Ener-G Egg Replacer
- 1/4 cup + 1 TB of water
- with any leafy greens (cracked by hands)
- or any other vegetable or you want!
- Optional toppings: salsa, ketchup, hot sauce, parsley, etc., combine
-

Instructions

- a small bowl all the ingredients collectively without the vegetables and non-essential vegetables.
- Let stand for 5 minutes. When too thick, add water. This is a pancake batter consistency (but no long-lasting much).
- Meanwhile, heat the non-stick pan on a low flame over medium heat. After the pan is hot, pour the batter into the pan as if you are making a pancake. Cover the pan with a lid and prepare dinner at low heat for 3 minutes until the edges are dry and bubbles form on the surface.
- Now mix the greens and/or veggies in one half of the omelet and take a spatula to fold the omelet in half and cook uncovered for 2 minutes.

- Remove and transfer to a plate before topping with ketchup, salsa, hot sauce, etc.!

Cinnamon French Toast

Ingredients

- 1 cup + 1-2 teaspoons simple or vanilla unsaturated non-dairy milk
- 1 tbsp white chia seeds
- soaked 1/3 cup and cashew-free walnuts for choice
- 3/4 teaspoon cinnamon
- 1/2 - 1/2 spoon. Pure Vanilla Extracts

- 1/8 teaspoon sea salt
- whole bread of choice (whole-grain, gluten-free, etc.) Book

Instructions

- In the use of a blender or a handheld blender, milk puree (starting with 1 cup; book), chia, Cashews, cinnamon, vanilla extracts, and sea salt until very smooth and thick (it thickens as it swells a bit and chia).
- Prepare a nonstick skeleton via wiping with a touch of oil (you want a nonstick pan, or it will be a sticky phenomenon!).
- Heat the pan extremely hot for a few minutes, then reduce to medium / medium-high.
- Dip a piece of bread in the batter. Turnover and allow the chia to soak in the combination for a few moments, then take the area further away in the skillet. Repeat with other slices, frying 2 to 3 portions or more at a time, depending on the size of your skillet.
- Fry for 3-5 minutes on each side until light brown. Keep the heat high enough to get a proper sip/crust on the bread, however, limit it when it scorches.
- Note that the slices will be sticky until they are ready to fluff, so be patient. Repeat until all the bread has been used. Serve with sparkling fruit and pure maple syrup.

Mango Lime Chia Pudding

Ingredients

- 1 15.5 oz coconut milk
- 3 cups or 10 oz sparkling or frozen mango
- chunks can take 1/4 cup maple syrup. I used grade A amber
- 1 tablespoon of mime zest, ground with a Microplane zesters.
- 1/4 cup freshly squeezed lime saffron

- 1/3 cup chia seeds
- 1/4 cup hemp seeds
- topping:
- mango, pineapple, banana or any fruit you would like with mango/lime

Instructions

- Coconut milk, mango chunks, Place in a blender and smooth the combo until the maple syrup, lemon zest, and lemon juice.
- Add the chia and hemp seeds to the blender and mix or blend less just to combine.
- You will have 4 cups of pudding, and you can like it again. I put 1/2 cup in each 1-pint jar for about eight servings, and then drink it with 1 cup of clean fruit for a total of 8 cups of sparkling fruit.
- As a note, if you use bananas to shorten your pudding, you will like to wait until you are ready to prepare it before adding the banana so that it browns. And do not touch the beige.
- Chill to set at least four hours, until the pudding is ready to eat. This pudding will last for 5-7 days.

Chocolate Waffle Fruit Pizza

Ingredients

- Waffle
- 1 Ripe Banana
- 1 Cup Gluten-Free Flour (or Grits)
- 1 Cup Non-Dairy Milk
- 2 tsp Baking Powder
- CHOCOLATE SAUCE
- 2 Ripe Bananas
- 2 Tablespoons Cocoa Powder (or Cocoa Powder)
- TOPPINGS: Strawberry (Raspberries,) Blueberries, Bananas, Kiwis, etc.)

Instructions

- Waffles for: Blend all the ingredients to make a thick batter.
- Prepare them according to your waffle maker's instructions. This makes about three 6-inch waffles in my waffle maker.
- For Chocolate: Whisk the bananas and cocoa in large quantities until creamy.
- Spread the sauce over the waffle, a peak with the fruit, enjoy!

Vegetarian Super Breakfast Bar

Ingredients

- 1.5 cups (180 grams) of mulberry and goji berry mixture, soaked in lukewarm water for about 30 minutes
- 4 apples
- 1 cup (240 ml) all-natural apple juice + three tablespoons divided.
- Teaspoon sunflower seed butter

- 2-22Tbsp maple syrup
- 4 cups (400 g) gluten-free license oats
- 2 tablespoons aluminum-free baking powder
- cinnamon (optional)
- large handful of sunflower seeds for garnish

Instructions

- Preheat oven to 390 ° F (200 ° C) and a baking dish (about 11 x 8 in) with prepared parchment paper.
- Finely chop the apple and remove the seeds. Add to a blender with 1 cup of apple juice. Process until smooth.

- The last three TBS mix sunflower butter with a creamy and clean paste with apple juice and maple syrup.
- In a bowl, mix oats, soaked (and dried) berries, sunflower paste, baking powder, and apple mixture.
- Press the dough into the dish with your arms or a spatula, sprinkled with sunflower seeds. Bake for about 20 minutes! As a pleasure!

Red Pesto and Black Oatmeal

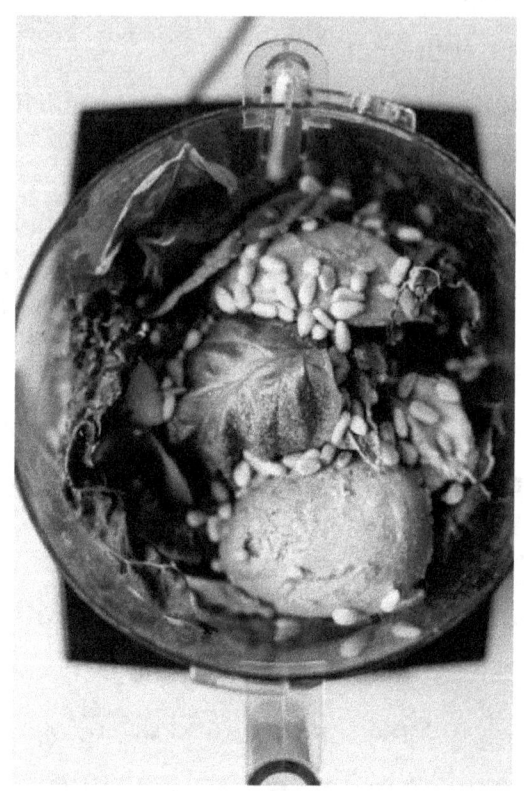

Ingredients

- JunkCouscous Cup of
- Half Cup Half Cup
- Veggie List (or water) 1,5-2 cups of
- 1,5 teaspoons dried teaspoon dried basil
- oregano 1chopped cabbage 1 cup

- chopped cherry 1 cup of tomatoes
- 1 onion
- 1 teaspoon tahini
- 1 big of your choice spoon pesto (I sun-dried tomato-walnut used pesto)
- 2 tablespoons food yeast
- 1 seed tbsp pumpkin
- 1 tablespoon of
- seeds, salt, pepper

Instructions

- oats, couscous, vegetable session Talk, parsley, basil, salt, and salt. Put black pepper in a small pot and prepare dinner over medium heat for 5 minutes periodically.
- When the oatmeal is smooth and mixes the chopped crust, tomatoes and chopped bananas in the cream (save a bit for decoration), Cook for another minute, then stir in the tahini, pesto, and nutritional yeast.
- Serve the porridge hot, with a little bit of cherry, cherry tomatoes, and pumpkin seeds! As a pleasure!

Peanut Butter and Jam Oatmeal

Ingredients

- Peanut Butter Granola
- of Cups Mix any nuts, seeds or coconut
- 1 tbsp peanut butter
- 1 tsp any light-colored sweetener, such as rice malt syrup or maple sesame
- raspberry chia jam

- ¼ cup raspberry
- 1 tbsp chia seed
- porridge.
- 2/3 cup rolled oats
- 1 plant cup plant-based milk, such as almonds, soy or coconut
- 2 tablespoons peanut butter (optional)
- 1 mashed banana (optional)
- other toppings
- 2 tablespoons peanut butter
- whatever you wish! For example, cocoa nibs, coconut syrup, coconut, and frozen berries

Instructions

- Preheat oven to 180 ° C.
- For the granola: Combine all ingredients in a bowl and unfold on a lined baking sheet — Bake for 10 minutes or until golden brown.
- Meanwhile, for raspberry chia jam: mash the raspberries with a fork and add through chia seeds.
- Meanwhile, for the oatmeal: Add all the ingredients in a small saucepan over high heat. Bring to a boil for 2 minutes and reduce it to a boil. Stir the oatmeal to make it positive it will not stick to the backside of the saucepan

when the oatmeal has reached your preferred consistency, set aside in 2 bowls.

- Garnish 2 bowls with granola, chia jam, extra peanut butter, and any other topping as desired! As a pleasure!

Kabuli Gram Flour Scramble Breakfast Recipe

Ingredients

- Kabuli Gram Flour Batter:
- 1/2 cup (60 g) Chickpea flour or use half cup + 1 or 2 Karachi maximum gram flour/gram flour
- 1/2 cup (125 ml) water
- 1 teaspoon nutritional yeast
- 1 teaspoon flaxseed meal
- 1/2 tsp (0.5 tsp) baking powder
- 1/4 tsp (0.25 tsp) salt

- 1/4 tsp (0.25 tsp) turmeric
- 1/4 tsp (0.25 tsp) or very little paprika
- 1 / 8 tsp (0.13 tsp). Black salt of black salted Indian sulfur, salted vegetable for a delicious taste
- pepper
- 1in 1 teaspoon oil
- clove garlic
- 1/4 cup (40 grams) chopped onion
- 2 teaspoons every asparagus, inexperienced bell pepper, zucchini, or individually Vegetable.
- 1/2 (0.5) inexperienced
- 2 tablespoons chopped Purple vine paper or tomato
- cilantro and pepper to garnish, keep

Instructions

- All the ingredients of the under a chickpea flour and keep aside. You can also use a lentil solution from my lentil frittata.
- Heat half a teaspoon of oil in a pan over medium heat. Add onion and garlic and cook until translucent. 3 minutes.
- Cook the veggies, chiles, and dinner for another 2 minutes.
- Mix in pink bell peppers or tomatoes and mix. At this point, you may want to add some spices or blends or some chopped greens.

- Add chickpea flour solution over the wedge. Cook for 2 minutes or so until the edges begin to set. Drizzle on the edges 1/2 teaspoon of oil. Scramble the mixture and proceed to cook. The mixture will be messy and dry. Scrap the backpack and prepare it for dinner for 2 minutes or so, compared to rubbing beforehand. Continue preparing dinner until the edges begin to dry. Total 4 to 5 minutes depending on your range and pan.
- Allow the flour mixture to warm for 1-2 minutes. Then break into small pieces. Sprinkle black pepper very generously. Sprinkle a little salt and garnish with cilantro (optional). Serve in multigrain toast or tacos or burritos.

Vegan Salmon Bagel

Ingredients

- 7 large carrots
- 2 cups of water
- ½ cup apple cider vinegar
- 2-3 tablespoons white miso
- 1 tsp. Liquid Smoke
- 1 Fist Algae (I use Vacuum)
- Dill and Chives
- 1 tbsp Copper
- Red Onion

- Vegetarian Cream Cheese
- 4 Bags
- Salt, Pepper

Instruction

- Preheat the oven to 200 ° C / 400 ° F.
- Peel carrots, then using a vegetable peel cut the carrots into long and thin strips. Try to reduce them as thin as possible.
- Add water, apple cider vinegar, miso, liquid smoke, algae, and freshly ground black pepper to a blender.
- Place the carrot strips in a casserole dish, pour the marinade, and shake so that it is fully coated.
- Cover the carrots with foil and bake for 15-20 minutes, then reduce the heat to 100 ° C / 210°F and cook the dinner for about 45 additional minutes.
- Baking time depends on the thickness of your carrot slices. Carrots need to be soft, but not meaty.
- Cool the carrots a little if needed, and serve bagels with cream cheese, dill, chives, onions, and capers if needed! As a pleasure!

Vegetarian Chocolate Zoot's

Ingredients

- 1/2 cup oats
- 1 cup chopped I have a medium zucchini
- 1 cup almond or oat milk
- 1 banana,
- 1 tbsp cocoa powder
- (using a spoon) (using)
- 22 tbsp chia seeds
- used for 6 tbsp plants. -Bed Milk For

- Topping:
- Fresh Berries
- Kiwi
- Banana
- Coconut Flakes
- Almond Butter
- Dark Chocolate, chopped
-

Instructions

- Pour chia seeds into a small bowl and stir in 6 tablespoons of plant-based milk. When you make the poet's relaxation, let it thicken.
- Place oats, chopped zucchini, and almond or oat milk in a small pot and prepare dinner for about 5 minutes over medium heat.
- Then use mashed bananas, cacao, soaked chia seeds, and incense sticks.
- Pour into two bowls and top it off with fresh berries (I used blueberries and raspberries), bananas, kiwi, almond butter, coconut flakes, and sliced dark chocolate.

Chapter 4: Plant-Based Lunch Recipes

Kaput Tabbouleh Salad

Ingredients

- 1 cup uncooked Kaput wheat
- 4 cups of water
- 1/2 small red onion
- 1 lemon (1 tbsp.)
- 11 Beefsteak tomatoes (or 2 plum / Roma tomatoes)

- 1 cup of leaves (1 bunch of sparkling Parsley)
- 1/4 cup fresh mint leaves, finely chopped
- 1cucumber
- tbsp2 tablespoons olive oil
- salt and pepper, to taste (1/4 - half a teaspoon each)

Instructions

- Cook the kaput wheat according to the package instructions, and total Please Stir it in cold water till it cools. I choose to cook kaput in extra water, and then dry the water in a colander pasta-style and rinse until it cools. kaput takes about 30 minutes to cook.

- While the kaput cooks, prepare a salad: chop the pink onion well. In a large bowl, mix dried crimson onion and lemon juice and let it marinate until you put the other vegetables together.

- Dip the tomatoes and set them in a colander to extract more juice. Discard the juice. Cut the cucumber in half lengthwise and use a spoon to scoop out the seeds. Discard the seeds. Cut the cucumber into small half-inch pieces. Finely chop parsley and mint leaves.

- Add chilled Kamut to a large bowl, cooked with the onion. Add the rest of the vegetables, chopped parsley and mint, and olive oil and mix well. Season with salt and pepper, to taste (start about 1/4 teaspoon each and go from there).

Greek Orzo Pasta Salad

Ingredients

- 8 oz Orzo Pasta
- 1 cup cherry tomatoes, chopped
- 1 cup English cucumber, chopped
- 1/2 cup pink onions
- , thinly sliced 1/3 cup kalamata olive Hua, chopped
- 1/4 cup cheese 1/4

- cup chopped
- 1/3 cup olive oil
- 1/4 cup red wine vinegar
- 1 lemon, fresh-squeezed juice
- 1 ½ teaspoon Oregano Pike
- 1/2 teaspoon kosher salt
- 1/2 teaspoon Taja Kali Mirch Min

instructions

- was parsley, a small pasta dish Menu instructions pasta and cooked al Dente. Remove from heat, drain, rinse pasta, then set aside.
- In a small bowl, whisk together olive oil, purple wine vinegar, lemon juice, parsley, salt, and pepper.
- In a large mixing bowl, add all components, including vinaigrette. Ensure that all ingredients are combined. Keep in the refrigerator for at least one hour to marinate.

Mexican Mason Jar Salad

Ingredients

- 1 cup of Salsa
- 1 cup Cooked Kidney Beans
- 3/4 Cup Cooked Candy Corn
- 1 Medium-sized Avocado About
- 8-10 Olives
- Handful
- of Lettuce Baked Tortilla Chips as required

- Salt & amp; Black pepper to taste
- Lime
- Ingredients For salsa
- 1 medium-sized tomato finely chopped
- 1 Crimson onion finely chopped
- salt & amp; to taste black pepper
- 1 tsp chopped coriander
- 1 tsp olive oil
- lemon juice

Instructions

- Salsa, mix onions, tomatoes, coriander, a pinch of salt & amp; Black pepper, olive oil, and lemon juice thoroughly. Stir to mix and set it aside

- Avocado Layer To put the avocado layer together, roughly mash the avocado with a fork. Squeeze some lemon juice with salt and stir to combine.
- lettuce
- Cut skinny strips of lettuce leaves and set it aside.
- Tortilla chips
- brushed with 2 corn tortillas oil and cut into triangles.
- Bake in a preheated oven at 190C for 8-9 minutes, turning just as in the middle.

- Mexican Salad Jarjari Utah
- layer on the bottom of the salsa.
- Top it with a layer of cooked kidney beans, sweetcorn, and then avocado guacamole mixer.
- Add olives, lettuce, and mix it with lots of baked tortilla chips.

Mediterranean Penne Pasta Salad

Ingredients

- 3 bell peppers chopped into small portions (1 green, 1 yellow, 1 crimson if possible) Australia = capsicum
- 1 Toni chopped (I then quarter each slice.)
- 1 sliced into small cubes
- eggplant, sliced 7 oz mushrooms small parts (I mixed-used four medium brown mushrooms) Class9
- ounces cherry tomatoes, oil, half
- olive cooking
- 10.5 oz Penne pasta dry
- 2/3 cup pesto
- 4 tablespoons Greek yogurt non-essentials - a cream for!

- cup roasted pine nuts (pre-purchase toast, or gently toast the pan in a dry, shaking each and every now and again)
- fall feta cheese
- a little chopped clean mint

Instructions

- Preheat the oven to 430F / 220C.
- Line 2 to three large-scale baking trays with baking paper and scatter all the vegetables except the tomatoes in a single layer on top of the baking tray.
- Drizzle with a little olive oil, then toss well with your hands. Sprinkle with lots of salt and pepper, then fry for 15 minutes.
- Add tomatoes to the tray. Roast for another 15 to 20 minutes until it is barely brown and caramelized.
- Meanwhile, prepare pasta according to bundle guidelines (8 to 10 minutes).
- Dry the pasta and tip it into a huge bowl. Tip in greens and stir through pesto and yogurt (if using).
- Sprinkle with pine nuts, feta, and mint.

Chickpea and Quinoa Salad with Honey Walnut Dressing

Ingredients

- 1/2 can be cooked Chickpeas
- 1 Bell Tomato
- 1/2 Red Onion
- 1/4 Butternut Squash Peeled and Cubed

- 1/2 Cup Quinoa
- 125 grams Halloumi
- 2 Tablespoons Olive Oil
- 1 Tablespoon Paprika
- 1 Avocado
- Stock Pot
- 3 Tbsp Honey
- 1/21/2 cup Walnuts
- 1 cup Parsley
- 1 Bird's Eye Chili

Instructions

- Heat your oven to 200 degrees' squash in
- butternut Toss the2 olive oil and 2 tablespoons of paprika. Fry for 35 minutes, letting it cook until it softens, then rub your quinoa in a sieve until the water dries, transfer it to a small pot and add 1 cup of water with some sea salt. Add more weather. Bring it to a boil, cowl it, and turn the heat to medium. Allow it to boil until the water is absorbed. Usually, it takes about 15-20 minutes. Once cooked, take it off the heat and fill it with a fork. Separately onion and tomato into a square chop the pieces. Cut the cinnamon into slices, dry and set aside to heat. Add a tablespoon of a large frying pan smoked paprika to 2 tablespoons of oil and fry the onions gently.

- When they become soft, then release the chickpeas and tomatoes, stir and cover. Reduce the warmth and allow the tomatoes to soften and roast in the roasted squash and cooked quinoa and melt in the melted inventory pot and thoroughly. Salt and pepper with for Sin Sward

- up avocado Chop Awr Men combine it pan halloumi and fry until it is golden on all aspects Slinky served on top Honey Akrotdresing roughly Prkat walnuts, parsley Warmer

- Shaman Mics a small dressing pan Gr Mike seconds the shed

- Take salad Pork Pagan, and enjoy!

Chana Masala | Easy

Ingredients

- 3 tablespoons avocado, canola or vegetable oil
- 1 giant onion, finely chopped (about 9 oz / 250 g)
- 2 tablespoons ground black pepper (chili flakes)
- 2 tablespoons ground cumin
- 2 tablespoon coriander
- 1/2 tablespoon flour Turmeric
- 2 Baker. Leaves

- 2 cardamom pods
- 4-6 garlic cloves, minced
- 2 tablespoons clean ginger, minced
- 2 small cans (15 oz / 425 g.) Chickpeas drained and rinsed Note: To keep one can of whole chickpeas and use a fork to almost crushing the chickpeas from the second can.
- 2 cups clear vegetable broth
- 1 small (15 oz / 425 g) overwhelmed tomato
- 1 1/2 teaspoon salt 1
- lemon or small lemon juice (whichever you prefer)
- a handful of fresh cilantros, roughly chopped
- 1 teaspoon spice
- heated serving(optional))
- Steamed rice (basmati rice is our favorite!)
- roughly chopped pumpkin, onion slices, Julienne ginger, fresh lime or Keka lemon juice Niched Dalen

Instructions

- oil and Yaj to medium heat a large pot, saute onion until soft (about 8 minutes). Sprinkle in chili flakes, cumin, coriander, turmeric, bay leaves, and cardamom pods, cook until the spices are fragrant (about 2-3 minutes). Stir in the minced garlic and ginger and any other sauce for 2-3 minutes.

- Pour in chickpeas, vegetable broth, heavy tomatoes, and salt, then stir well.
- Increase the heat and bring the chana masala to a boil, then reduce to a boil and cook for 10 minutes, stirring occasionally.
- Add lemon/lime juice, Cetaphil, and garam masala. Taste and regulate seasonings as required.

Instant Pot Kuban Black Beans and Rice

Ingredients

- 1 Tbsp Olive Oil
- 1 Medium Crimson or Yellow Bell Pepper,
- 4 Cloves Garlic, Minced
- 1 Tablespoon Onion (Reserve 2for Garnish)
- Tbsp2 Tablespoons Cumin Seeds
- 1½ Tablespoons Dried Parsley
- 11 tablespoons. Wine Vinegar
- 3 Cups Vegetable Broth
- 1/2 Cups Dry White Cooking Wine (Or Extra Broth)
- 1 Cups Dry Black Beans,

- 3/4 Cups Long Grain Brown Rice
- 2 Tablespoons Lime Juice
- 1 Avocado, Cubed
- 1 Bona Tomato, Decide
- Fresh Cilantro or Garnishee to Parsley

Instructions

- sauté set your stress cooker and add oil, capsicum, garlic, and purple onion, reserving 2 tbsp of purple onion for garnish.
- Stir occasionally for 5 minutes.
- Add cumin, parsley, and purple wine vinegar and cook for 2 minutes.
- Add broth, cooking wine, black beans, and rice.
- Cover dinner and cook for 30 minutes.
- While the beans are cooking, combine the chopped tomatoes, lemon juice, avocado, and onion in a bowl.
- Release pressure naturally for about 10 minutes, then search for pot.
- If the beans are still a little hard, put the lid back on for 5–10 minutes.
- Divide into bowls and top with avocado mixture.

Vegetarian Chicken Curry Salad Sandwich for Chloe Curry Salad

Ingredients

- 1 tbsp coconut oil (or sub vegetable or rapeseed oil)
- 1 onion,
- 1 tsp curry powder, to taste.

- 400 grams (14 oz) of tinned, dried and rinsed
- 50% (1/3 cup) uncooked cashews ** - Soak in cold water a day or in boiling water for 10 minutes.
- 2 teaspoons lemon juice
- 1 teaspoon mango chutney (or sub agave or maple syrup
-). Coarsely chopped (or sub 1 teaspoon dried coriander)
- 2 tablespoons dehydrated coconut
- salt + pepper,
- to taste:
- gall bread, flatbread, sandwich bread (gluten-free if necessary)
- Salad leaf leaves
- red chili, Tilionco reduced

Instruction

- Lincoln curry salad Menaces:
- Heat oil in a frying pan and onion amphora hot time and
- Cook 10 minutes. Until soft and slightly caramelized
- Cook. Add curry powder and fry for a minute until fragrant
- Mash breaks into a hard knuckle with chana fork or potato masher.
- Add the chickpeas to the frying pan and fry for another two minutes until it is heated through the medium, transfer bowl, and add a cashew nut to a blender or food processor (Stick in one hand). The blender also works well) and is

definitely smooth, including a slight splash of water until you achieve your desired consistency - it needs to last quite a bit, but not too much water Is. Add the mixed cashews to the bowl along with the chickpeas and add lemon juice, mango chutney., Coriander, Boiled Coconut and Salt + Pepper

- Mix properly to taste and change the taste and modify the season as necessary.

Chickpeas Wraps

Ingredients

- 4 large flour tortillas
- 1 roasted chickpea
- Vegan BBQ4 tablespoons BBQ sauce
- 4 tablespoons yogurt, or veg mayo
- 4 leaves green leaves salad, chopped
- 1 tomato, chopped

- only lemon, only juice, optional

Instructions

- This recipe Prepare oven-roasted chickpeas according to. This will take you at least 30 minutes but can be prepared in advance.
- Heat a pan and do not cook every aspect of the tortilla for more than a minute. You only like to heat it and do not prepare dinner until it becomes brown and stiff. You can also do it in the microwave or oven, test the label accordingly.
- Place sliced lettuce, tomatoes, chickpeas, BBQ sauce, and yogurt in the middle of each tortilla. Drizzle with lemon juice.
- Fold (1 "/ 2cm) on each side of the tortilla. Initially, roll it up tightly from one end until you have a good wrap. Cut in half and serve.

Hummus with Crushed Pocket

Ingredients

- 1 eggplant
- 2 carrots
- 1 purple vine paper
- 1 tablespoon juice-el.
- 1 tablespoon turmeric
- 1/2 teaspoon Candy paprika
- 1/4 teaspoon fresh bottom pepper
- 1/4 teaspoon sea salt
- 4 loaves crushed bread preferably

- 1 cup or one hundred and sixty grams Perfect Great Store - Homemade Hums Bought or Homemade Hummus, see ingredient list below
- handful Spinach
- pomegranate seeds,
- sliced Ajmo the
- Gahan Shishra brought to lukewarm:
- 1 Cup or 160 grams' chickpeas
- juice half a lemon juice
- 1 tbsp tahini paste
- 1 small garlic clove
- 3 tablespoons virgin olive oil
- 1/2 teaspoon floor cumin
- 1/2 teaspoon juice-el (optional) paprika (optional)
- 1 / 2 teaspoons turmeric (optional)
- 1/4 teaspoon sweet
- pepper flakes (optional))
- 2 tablespoons water starts with 1 tablespoon, then continue adding 1 tablespoon at a time when it is favored.
- land time for tasting the chili pepper

Instructions

- Preheat to 200 ° C or 400 ° F. Julienne Your Vegetable: Cut eggplant, carrots, and bell peppers into 10 cm (4 inches) long strips and arrange them on a baking tray sprinkled with cooking spray. Sprinkle with spices (preferably mix them together in a small bowl), salt and pepper and fry for about 25 minutes or until the eggplants are tender.

- Meanwhile, if you want to make it yourself, make hummus. Mix all the ingredients except water and mix until smooth. Add water, 1 tbsp at a time until desired consistency.

- Bake Pita Bread as per guidance on the package deal and reduce them in half. They will structure the pockets, so you can fill them with about 2 tablespoons of hummus, a few strips of each roasted vegetable, and a few leaves of baby spinach.

- Finally, sprinkle your pyre pocket with pomegranate seeds and chopped parsley. If you don't follow a vegetarian diet, drizzling them with a bit of Greek yogurt is great.! As a pleasure!

Broccoli Slaw Veggie Wrap with Spicy Hummus

Ingredients

- 1 Tortilla (your favorite) (gluten-free, if necessary)
- 3-4 tablespoons of Spiced Hummus (or preferred to save your sold hummus and combine with a few tablespoons of salsa)
- a few leaves of Romaine Lettuce or Sparkling Spinach (or leafy green of your choice)
- 1/2 cup Broccoli Slavic
- 1/4 apple (thin)

- 2 tsp Dairy Free Plain Unsweetened Yogurt
- 1/2 tsp Clear Lemon Juice
- Salt & amp; Black pepper (to taste)

Instructions

- Mix yogurt and lemon juice with broccoli. Add a sprinkle of salt and pepper to taste, and mix well. To cancel.
- Lay the tortilla flat.
- Spread spicy hummus around the tortilla.
- Spread the latest on top of the spiced hummus.
- On one half, stack the broccoli slaw on lettuce.
- Place the apple slices on top of the slab.
- Fold the sides of the tortilla and then, starting with the quail that has the Slavs and apples, roll tightly.
- Cut into 1/2 and enjoy!

Sandwich Vegetarian Eggplant Sandwich

Ingredients

- 1 eggplant medium size, peeled, chopped and pre-soaked in slightly salted water
- 2 panini or ciabatta buns
- 4 tablespoons vegetarian mayo
- 1 tomato chopped
- 1/2 cucumber chopped
- 1/2 cup Rocket or Arugula
- . Marinade:
- 1 tablespoon olive oil
- 1 tablespoon soy sauce or gluten-free tamarind sauce for

- 1 tablespoon egg view syrup or maple syrup
- 1 tsp smoked paprika
- 1/4 tsp salt
- 1/4 tsp floor pepper

Instructions

- To make eggplant For Eggplant Mix ingredients in a small bowl, then brush the pickle on the eggplant slices. Bake on a baking sheet for 20 minutes or so, or shallow fry, and dry on kitchen towel paper.
- To make a sandwich:
- Start by cutting the panini or ciabatta bread in half lengthwise.
- Spread a layer of vegan mayonnaise, add a layer of smoky eggplant slices, tomato slices, cucumber slices, a sprinkle of salt and pepper, and finally, the pinnacle with rocket/arugula leaves and the other half of the panini Cover with a portion or ciabatta bread.
- Cover with some foil, then toast the sandwich in a grill. Once you get it out, cut it in half (cut through the foil if you are going to finish it immediately. Or pack it in a foil to take to work, go for a picnic or just later Get.

Chapter 5: Plant-Based Snacks Recipes

Maple-Pumpkin Vegan Quesadilla

Ingredients

- 1 Medium to large casing or tortilla, any variety (if using small tortillas, use two.
- 1 teaspoon more virgin olive oil
- 1/4 cup or 1-piece vegan cheese, chopped The
- 1/4 cup cooked white part. beans - or 1 tablespoon

- 1 tablespoon parsley, finely chopped (optional) piece of
- pumpkin butter - have left Hushing:
- 1 cup pumpkin puree, unsaturated
- 1 tablespoon maple syrup
- 1 teaspoon Vegan butt Su, melted or softened
- pinch of salt
- 1/8 teaspoon pumpkin pie spice or cinnamon zest
- pinch of clean orange(optional)

Instructions

- Add all the pumpkin butter components to a blender with a. Clean and warm slightly to low. Scoop into an aspect bowl.
- in a skillet heat the extreme heat. Add olive oil. pan and distribute the oil evenly to swirl the pan.
- pumpkin a coming of the interior of the tortilla in butternut part. Using a fork, break the beans in the pumpkin. If using hummus, slayer it on the other half of the interior. Parsley. Parsley and Sprinkle in cheese. If using a piece of cheese, tear it into small pieces.
- Place the tortilla in the pan and allow the backyard to sizzle in hot oil for 1-3 minutes,
- until the edges turn brown, although the tortilla is still tender enough to bend. Fold the tortilla to close. Cover the pan with a lid for 1-2 minutes to melt the cheese.

- The tortilla has to bark and fizzle through now, and warm and soft interiors. Remove the quesadilla from the pan. Slice into triangles and serve hot.

Hot Pumpkin Mug

Ingredients

- Sunleaded
- 1 1/4 cups non-dairy milk
- 1 Tbsp pumpkin puree,
- 1/4 tsp Pumpkin Pie Masala
- (Add extra spices if desired: cinnamon, nutmeg, ginger, turmeric, cayenne)
- 1 / 8 tsp or a few drops of vanilla extract (opt)
- 1 - 3 tsp maple syrup (depending on how you like the candy)

- pinch of sea salt
- topping: soy or coconut whip

Instructions

- all ingredients except maple syrup Add to blender Switch to. Blend to low as usual. Some pumpkin lumps are fine. Room Temple Pumpkin mixes more easily.
- Pour mixture into a small saucepot. Bring to a boil and then reduce to medium and able to soften until any small clumps of pumpkin in the hot liquid. Immerse for about 2-4 minutes.
- Transfer the returned combination to the blender, adding the maple syrup and combo to the fruity at least once.
- Pour into a serving mug and whip non-essential soy or coconut whip and pumpkin spices or a sprinkle of cinnamon or nutmeg.
- Serve hot and steamy. To quickly reheat or reheat, a few seconds in the microwave can do this.

Hummus Zucchini Roll-Ups

Ingredients

- 1 medium zucchini
- 1/2 cup Sabra Sun-Dried Tomato Hums afar
- 1/2 cup quinoa tablespoons of a spoon
- 1/4 cup fresh parsley
- 8 - 10basil
- 1/4 cup finely chopped red chili *

- 1/4 cup finely chopped. Carrots *

Instructions

- Using a mandolin slicer, use zucchini-length slices in skinny strips (you want half or eight - 10 slices of zucchini all over; the rest of the store is made of a sauté or my farmers market of quinoa salad for!).
- In a small bowl, collect hummus and quinoa collectively. Spread about 1 tablespoon of the filling on zucchini and spread it evenly with your fingers (or a spoon).
- Arrange the herbs at one end, pinnacle with veins, and then roll the zucchini like sushi. If necessary, secure the end with toothpicks.
- Repeat until all components are used.
- Serve once and Enjoy!

Copycat Brad's Raw Cheese Broccoli Popper

Ingredients

- 4 cups broccoli florets, washed and 1in 1-inch pieces,
- cup unsalted cashews overnight (or at least 4 hours) cup
- soaked1 red bell pepper, seeded and sliced

- 2 TB freshly squeezed lemon juice.

- 1/8 cup water

- 2 heaping TB Dietary yeast

- 1/4 tsp onion powder

- 1/4 tsp turmeric powder

- 1/8 tsp Good sea salt

Instructions

- Fry cashews and add to a food processor or high-speed blender. Pour for 30 seconds. Scrap the sides of the container with a spatula.

- Keep the chopped purple chilies in the container. Process two for another 30 seconds. Re-scrap the aspects of the container.

- Add lemon juice, water, nutritional yeast, onion powder, turmeric powder, and sea salt to the container — process until generally smooth, or for about 45 seconds.

- Place the broccoli in a huge bowl. Add the paneer cashew mixture to two bowls. Gently twist the broccoli and "cheese" collectively, and each piece of broccoli is well coated with a mixture of cashew nuts of cheese.

- Place the broccoli portions on your dehydration tray, being careful to ensure that they no longer contact each other.

- Follow your dehydration guidelines and dehydrate at one hundred and twenty-five levels for about 8 hours or until crisp.
- Store in an air-tight container to maintain freshness.

Chocolate Chip Cookie Dough Bars - No Bake

Ingredients

- 2 tablespoons coconut oil
- 2 tbsp almond milk or other non-dairy milk
- 1/4 cup (40 grams) coconut palm sugar or brown sugar
- 1 tbsp vanilla extract 2 tsp much less severe to taste.
- 1/4 tsp (0.25 tsp) salt
- 3/4 cup (90 g) grits licensed of finely ground oats, or any mildly flavored cereal flour / white flour
- 3/4 cup (84 g) almonds of use flour / fine powder

- 1 /. 4 cups (59.15 grams) of raw sugar is very less sweet and less
- than 1/3 to half a cup (60 to ninety grams) are vegetarian. Enjoy Life Mini Chocolate Chips or Vegan Chocolate through Theo to make it free of palm oil.

Instructions

- Melt coconut oil through heating in a pan or bowl. Almond milk, coconut sugar, and vanilla until well combined.
- Add flour, salt, and powdered sugar and mix. Taste and adjust the candy if necessary, or add more flour or oil for smooth, sticky dough, although not too sticky dough. Do not add too much flour as the doe sets and cool them. Fold in chocolate chips and mix.
- Press on a parchment sheet and a half-inch thick rectangle (eight with the help of about 7-inch size) and refrigerate until set. Cut the bars and save in a hermetically placed container in the fridge, if any are left for the next day :). Eat as, or add to these ice creams, morning porridge or chia pudding, shakes, and whatnot.

No-Bake Gluten-Free Vegan Apple Crumb Bars

Ingredients

- Crust and 1 Half Cup Full Pecan Toasted is fantastic, although toasted is just fine with
- 1 half-cup gluten-free oats that you can regularly use historical oats.
- 1/2 teaspoon kosher salt 1/2 teaspoon
- cinnamon

- 1/3 cup pack chopped prunes
- 1/4 cup coconut oil solid, not melted
- .to fill,
- 2 giant granny apples peeled, cored, and finely diced
- 3 tablespoons dark brown sugar
- 1/2 teaspoon cinnamon
- 2 teaspoons cornstarch
- / 2 cups water

Instructions

- An 8 x 8-inch baking pan with foil so that it spreads to the sides. Line the bottom of the pan with a square of parchment paper.
- To make the crust and toppings, combine pecans, oats, salt, and cinnamon in a food processor and stir until thickly ground. Add prunes and pulse until well combined. Add coconut oil and lentils until the combination looks sticky and moist. Pinch something between your fingers - it should feel soft, not sandy. If it is too dry, add a tablespoon of coconut oil. Transfer a little extra by half of the combination into the organized pan, burning the rest. With clean hands, press it firmly and evenly toward the back of the pan.
- For the filling, combine apples, brown sugar, and cinnamon in a medium saucepan. In a small bowl, water the cornstarch and the mixture. Pour over the apple. Bring

to a boil, then reduce heat and boil until the combination thickens and apples are tender but still hold their shape for 15 to 20 minutes.

- Spread the apple filling evenly over the crust in the pan. Pour the pecans mixture over the apple and press gently. Transfer the pan to the refrigerator and be very firm for at least 4 hours.

- Using the foil as a handle, take the entire piece out of the pan and cut it into bars. Store the bar in the refrigerator.

Cherry Pie Tarts

Ingredients

Filling Ingredients

- 4 cups cherries (about 1 lb., pitted)
- 1/4 cup maple syrup
- 1 tbsp white whole wheat flour

- crust
- 4 1/4 cups white whole wheat flour
- 1 coconut oil softens
- 2 Material for tsp salt
- 2 tbsp maple syrup
- Boil 1 cup of bloodless water.

Instructions

- In a medium pot, add cherry co and 1/4 cup maple syrup over medium-low heat for 12-15 minutes until the cherry is tender. Sprinkle in the flour and cook the dinner for another minute to thicken more. To cancel.
- Preheat the oven to 375 degrees.
- In a food processor, mix all crust components without water. Slowly add water through the top of the food processor as it is running. Turn off when water comes along with the flour. You are able to shape a ball of dough easily.
- On the dough work surface, roll the dough into a large, 1/8-inch-thick rectangle. Depending on your work surface, you may favor taking out half of the dough at a time.
- Cut the dough into 24 rectangles (3 inches by 5 inches each). Alternatively, you should use a cookie cutter to make different sizes, or you may want to cut it into smaller squares.

- Distribute 12 backside rectangles on 2 cookie sheets. Add about 2 tablespoons of filling to the middle area of each rectangle, leaving the edge of the room the edge of the dough should be part of the round pieces.
- Place the remaining 12 pieces of dough on the crest of the crumbled bottle, and press the edges with a fork.
- Bake for about 20 minutes, until the back of each tart turns light brown.
- Cool on a wire rack and keep in a hermetic container.

Vegetarian Chocolate Avocado Cookies

Ingredients

- 1 1/4 cups all-purpose flour
- 1 teaspoon baking powder
- ½ teaspoon of sea salt
- 2/3 cup Dutch-processed cocoa
- 1/4 cup coconut oil
- 1/4 cup mashed avocado
- 1/4 cup granulated sugar
- 1 / 2 cups brown sugar

- 1 teaspoon vanilla extract
- 1/3 cup almond milk
- ½ cup vegetarian chocolate chips

Instructions

- Heat the oven to 350 tier f. Separate a large baking sheet with a Silpat baking mat or parchment paper and set aside.
- In a medium bowl, whisk the flour, baking powder, salt, and cocoa collectively.
- In the bowl of a stand mixer, beat coconut oil, avocado, and sugar until creamy and smooth, about 2-3 minutes. Add vanilla extracts.
- With the mixer on low, add half of the flour mixture. Add milk and then the ultimate dry ingredients. Mix until the dough disappears. Stir in the chocolate chips.
- Pour the cooked dough into tablespoon balls and place them on an organized baking sheet, about 2 inches apart. Slightly flatten the cookies with the palm or spatula of your hand. Set the cookies for 10 minutes or around the edges, although still soft in the center. Allow cookies to cool for two minutes on a baking sheet. Transfer to a wire cooling rack and cool completely.

Cinnamon Maple Sweet Potato Bites

Ingredients

- 4 medium candy potatoes
- 3 tablespoons melted butter
- p tablespoons cornstarch
- 2-3 tablespoons maple syrup
- 1 tablespoon cinnamon Heat the

Instruction

- oven to 425 ° F. Line a baking sheet with parchment paper or foil and set aside.
- Peel the sweet potato and cut it into bite-size cubes with a sharp knife. Place cubes in a gallon-sized bag and drip into the melt seal the bag and provide it with a shake to coat all the pieces in butter.
- Add cornstarch, cinnamon, and maple syrup. Shake the bag some more and then transfer the bite to the organized baking sheet. Try to make sure that they do not stand on top of each other, so keep them all in the same layer. (You may also need two pans.)
- Sprinkle with cinnamon on the pan and surrounding space in a 25-30 oven, cutting about halfway through the baking time.
- Take the bites from the oven and allow them to cool for about 5 minutes before eating. Not only will this prevent you from burning your style buds into oblivion, but it will additionally cut off any other threats.

Fruit Salad Kebabs and Chocolate Sunflower Dip

Ingredients

- 4 kiwis, peeled and 1/4-inch slices into
- sliced into6 large strawberries, 1/4-inch slices into
- 1 large or 2 small bananas, peeled and sliced into 1/4-inch slices Better (less) ripe, so they don't brown too quickly)

- Sunflower balsamic dip (1 1/2 cups)120g
- 1/2 cup (70g) raw, unsalted sunflower kernels
- 1/2 cup () without Ripe apple juice
- 1 tbsp. Vinegar
- 2 teaspoons pure maple syrup
- 1/4 teaspoon fine sea salt
- 1/2 cup + 2 tablespoons water
- chocolate sunflower dip
- 1/2 cup (70 grams) uncooked, unsalted sunflower kernels
- 1/4 cup pure maple syrup
- 3 tbsp raw cacao Powder
- 1 /. 2 tablespoons vanilla extracts
- 2 tablespoons water
- pinch sea salt

Instructions

- Slide the fruit over the skewer, starting with the banana and end with the banana. I placed thirteen fruits on each dagger, which gave me 4 daggers. I used metal skewers in the photos, although they became much more rounded, so I would support the use of people in time. I did this later and they did better to take the plunge.

- To make a balsamic dip, add all the ingredients to a high-power blender or food processor and stir until completely smooth. Add flavor and any additional sweetener if you want it sweeter. If desired, keep a few moments in the fridge to kickback.

- To make a chocolate dip, you will want a food processor instead of a blender. It has very little water and does not work at all in a blender. I tried it and it just wouldn't blend and creamy. The food processor produced a smooth, silky texture. Just add sunflower kernels to the food processor. Process them into an excellent flour and then add the closing elements and the system until it becomes very smooth and creamy with more and more bits of sunflower kernels. This will take a few minutes and you will want to scrape the aspect once or twice — store at room temperature to keep a smooth texture.

Cherry Bakewell Cupcake

Ingredients

- 1/4 cup (30 grams) Tapioca Autogram) flour
- 1/3 cup (55 flour)
- 1/4 cup (35 of brown rice flour grams)
- 1/3 cup (40 grams) ground almonds
- 1 tsp baking
- 2 tsp xylitol
- 1 / 4 tsp pure stevia
- 3/4 cup () rice milk
- 1 almond extract

- 185 ml / tsp 6 tsp cherry jam (I used St. Delfour)

Instructions

- Put Tapioca Flour, Flour, Brow. Rice flour, ground almonds, baking powder, xylitol, and stevia in a large mixing bowl. Stir until well mixed. Then, mix in almond extracts and rice milk, and collectively use one hand until smooth. Mix.
- When this is done, line a muffin tray with 6 large cupcake cases. Then, add 2 tbsp of the cake combination in each case. Next, add 1 tablespoon of the cherry jam to the center of each case in Keep. Then, to cover the jam, pinnacle every cupcake with the final cake mixture. Pour the cupcakes into the oven and bake for about 30 minutes until golden.
- When the cupcakes are baked, put them off the oven and set them to cool completely. Then, serve when cooled.

Tahini Dark Chocolate Vegan Granola Bars

Ingredients

- Granola Bars
- 2 cups Gluten-Free Oats
- 1 Cup Brown Rice Cereal (I like Avon) Tsp
- 1 Cinnamon

- 1/4 Cup Flax Meal
- 2 Tbsp Chia Seeds
- 1/4 Cup Sunflower Seeds
- 1/4 Tsp Salt
- 1 / 2 cup tahini
- 1 teaspoon vanilla
- 2/3 cup of brown rice syrup
- 1-2 tablespoons of the non-dairy milk (I use soy) (as needed)
- 1/4 cup non-dairy chocolate chunks (Vakil Pic)
- Dark Chocolate Drizzle
- 1/2 cup non-dairy chocolate chips/chunks
- 1-3 tablespoons non-dairy milk
- pinch salt

Instructions

- oven to 325 Heats up to Tier F.
- Make an 8x8 pan lined with parchment paper (long enough for its ends to end) and set aside.
- In a huge bowl, mix oats, brown rice cereal, cinnamon, flax meal, chia, sunflower seeds, and salt. Mix well
- In a small bowl, collectively tahini, vanilla, and brown rice syrup. If the mixture thickens without any doubt, then add 1 tablespoon of non-dairy milk at a time and whisk again until the mixture becomes plastic.

- Add wet ingredients to the dry ingredients, while always stirring to mix well. Add chocolate chips, if using, and mix well.

- Once the entirety is well incorporated, pour the combination into an 8x8 pan. Press the mixture into a uniform layer with your fingers. This helps to wet your palms before pressing slightly.

- Cook for 25–28 minutes until it becomes golden and starts to mix. The bars will move to join as they cool.

- Cool in the pan on a wire rack for 10–15 minutes until you can spontaneously pull the bar out through the retaining end of the parchment paper. Continue cooling the bars on parchment paper on a wire rack for another 10 minutes. Cut into bars or squares and continue cooling if they still feel soft.

- Once the bars are completely cool, whisk the dark chocolate viscous in a double boiler until melted. Add 1 teaspoon of non-dairy milk at a time until the desired consistency is reached. You like it thin enough to drizzle, through thick enough to install on the bars. Drizzle on the bars.

Cereal Zucchini Chocolate Cupcakes

Ingredients

- Cupcake
- 1 small zucchini {about a cup chopped}, roughly chopped
- ¾ cup flour Kuku
- 8 smooth Medjool dates
- 8 teaspoons maple syrup
- cream from1 can of full-fat coconut milk {half a cup about}

- 6 tablespoons cocoa powder
- ¼ cup coconut water {or non-dairy milk or
- water}:
- Frosting 10 soft marrow Kjur Kakao
- 2 large Cmmc Powder
- 2 tablespoons maple syrup
- water cup water {or non-dairy milk}
- 1 teaspoon pure vanilla
- salt Eka dash
- topping
- Optional: cocoa nibs, dried mulberry, some shaved chocolate, or different toppings of your choice.

Instructions

- Preheat oven to 350F. Set aside a 6-cup muffin pan with cupcake liners.
- Put all the cupcakes in a blender and mix {a food processor also works for this}. Transfer to the pan, divide evenly and lift the batter all the way up, as long as you can without spreading it out.
- Bake in a preheated oven for about 45–55 minutes, or until a skewer inserted comes out the center clean. {Note: They will crack on the crest when cooked - and will be protected with frost anyway :)}. Remove from the oven and cool on a cooling rack.

- Prepare frosting by mixing all ingredients together in a blender until smooth. The frosting will become sticky, so spoon evenly over every cupcake and then unfold around. Top with your favorite toppings and enjoy!

Smoky Pinto Bean Tostadas

Ingredients

- 1/2 medium onion (diced)
- 1 / 3-1 / 2 cup vegetable broth (split)
- 1 garlic clove (minced)
- 1 teaspoon cumin

- 1 1/2 teaspoon smoked paprika
- 1/2 - 1 teaspoon Chili Powder (depending on your preference for heat)
- 2 15 oz can Pinto beans (dry)
- Dash of liquid smoke (optional)
- A squeeze of lime juice (optional)
- 8 Tostada shells
- Suggested topping:
- Half Cherry Tomato
- Castro
- Avocado Slice
- Dyed Jalapeno
- Dye Red Onion
- Chopped Radish.
- Salsa
- Vegetarian Butter Croft Shake the

Instructions

- Medium onion softened with 2 tablespoons of veggie broth, about 5 minutes. Keep an eye on it the whole time, and if the onion dries too much, then add a small spoon or veggie broth.
- Add garlic and sauté any other minute.

- Add spices and pinto beans. Mash all over with a potato masher or fork until desired consistency (I appreciated leaving some little chunky).
- Add any other tbsps. of veggie broth through the mixture and heat for 2 minutes, once more to the desired consistency. You don't do it in favor of smoothie, but it is moist, no longer a dry paste.
- If using and stir, add liquid smoke and/or a squeeze of lime juice.
- You should be good to go!

Vegetarian Cheese Popcorn

Ingredients

- 1 Tbsp Coconut Oil
- 1/4 cup equal to one cup Organic Popcorn Kernels 8 cups Popcorn
- Cheese Powder!
- One cup 1/3of raw cashew nuts
- teaspoon1 tablespoon turmeric
- 2 tablespoons + 2 spoons 10 grams' nutritious yeast
- 2 tablespoons cornstarch
- 1/4 teaspoon cumin
- 1 teaspoon salt

- 1 teaspoon dried minced onion

Instructions

- All cheese powder ingredients one meal. Add the processor and the lentils to the fine paneer. Powder forms. Do not process now!
- In a large stockpot, heat coconut oil with 3 popcorn kernels over high heat and cover. Once all 3 kernels pop up, cast them and add 1/4 of a cup of popcorn kernels.
- Place a lid on the stockpot and shake the pot occasionally. As soon as the popcorn starts to pop, keep stirring it. Once the popping slows down, heat the pot over, and remove the lid. Allow the popcorn to rest for 2 minutes.
- Take the popcorn hot (not hot!) And pour it into a large paper bag with 1/2 cup of cheese powder. Stir the bag until all the popcorn is coated. Add more cheese powder if needed.

Chapter 6: Plant-Based Dinner Recipes

Corn Salsa with Black Eyed Peas Cake

Ingredients

- 2 (15.5-oz) unsalted black-eyed peas, rinsed, drenched and split
- 1/2 cup whole-wheat Panko (Japanese breadcrumbs)

- 1/4 cup thinly sliced inexperienced onions, Divided
- 3/4 teaspoon kosher salt, split
- 1/8 teaspoon ground crimson pepper
- 2 large eggs, gently
- 2 tbsp olive oil, split divided
- 1 cup fresh or frozen corn kernels,
- 1/2 cup shaved cherry tomatoes 1
- 1/2 teaspoon Shrike
- 1 tbsp chopped clean flat-leaf parsley
- 1/4 teaspoon freshly ground black pepper

Instructions

- Put half a cup of peas in a bowl; To cancel. Place remaining peas in a food processor; Lentils until thick. In a bowl, mix mashed peas, pandora, 3 tablespoons onion, half a teaspoon salt, red chili, and eggs. Divide the pea mixture into eight (3-inch) patties.
- Heat 1 tbsp of oil in a large nonstick pan. Add four patties to the pan; Cook dinner 5 minutes on each side. Remove patty from pan; To keep safe. Repeat the system with the last 1 teaspoon of oil and the last four patties.
- Increase the heat to medium-high. Add corn to the pan; Prepare dinner for 2 minutes. Place corn in a bowl; Let stand for 5 minutes.

- Add reserved half cup of peas, chopped 1 tbsp of onions, stirring the last 1/4 teaspoon salt, tomatoes, and the ultimate ingredients to combine corn. Spoon evenly over cake.

Banh Mi Pizza

Ingredients

- 1 cup apple cider vinegar 1 cup water
- 1/2 cup granulated sugar
- 1/2 teaspoon kosher salt
- 1 cup match-cut carrots
- 1/2 English cucumber,
- finely chopped 1/3 cup finely chopped radish
- 1 / 2 clean jalapenos, seeded and finely chopped
- 12 oz. Fresh Deli Whole-wheat flour
- 1/2 teaspoon low-sodium soy sauce or tamari 1

- 1/2 tbsp sesame oil, 5 oz portion-skim mozzarella cheese, divided (about 1/4 cup)
- 1/2 Tablespoon canola. Mayonnaise
- 1/2 teaspoon Sriracha Chili Sauce
- 1/2 cup loosely fresh cilantro leaves it

Instructions

- Place a pizza stone or baking sheet in the oven. Preheat the oven to 500 ° F. (Do not add the pizza stone when the oven is preheated.)
- a saucepan, mix vinegar, 1 cup water, sugar, and salt. Bring to a boil on medium-high; Cook, occasionally stirring until sugar and salt have dissolved. Stir in carrots, cucumber, radish, and jalapeño. remove from heat; Let stand for 10 minutes. Drain and set aside.
- Roll the dough in a 13-inch circle on a large piece of parchment paper; Hole well with a fork. Brush soy sauce and 1 tbsp of sesame oil on the dough. Place the dough (on paper) on a preheated stone. Bake at 500 ° F for 6 minutes.
- Sprinkle mozzarella evenly over the dough. Bake at 500 ° F for 5 minutes.
- Add mayonnaise, sriracha, and remaining 1 1/2 teaspoons of sesame oil.
- Pour the pickle evenly over the pizza. The combination on top of drizzle. Spray with Sitaphal. Cut into eight slices.

Cauliflower with Sichuan Tofu

Ingredients

- 12 oz. Extra-firm tofu, dry and
- reduce to 3/4-inch. Cubes 3 tablespoons cornstarch, split
- 2 tablespoons canola oil 1 cup unsalted vegetable stock, split
- 3 tablespoons low-sodium soy sauce 1 tablespoon sherry vinegar 1
- 1/2 tablespoons hoisin sauce
- 3 cups cauliflower flowers
- 2 cups finely chopped diagonally celery

- 6 garlic cloves, finely chopped 1
- 1/2 tablespoons unsalted ketchup
- 1/2 teaspoon beaten crimson pepper
- 1/2 cup finely chopped green onions.

Instructions

- Pat the tofu dries with a paper towel. Place 7 tablespoons of cornstarch in a large bowl. Add tofu; toss to coat. Take the tofu out of the bowl. Heat the oil in a large nonstick pan on medium-high. Add tofu; Cook dinner for 6 minutes or until golden and crisp. Remove the tofu to a plate with a slotted spoon.
- Combine exactly 2 teaspoons of cornstarch and 1/4 cup of inventory in a bowl until smooth. Stir in 3/4 cup stock, soy sauce, vinegar, and hoisin to close.
- Add cauliflower to the oil locked in the pan; Cook dinner for three minutes or until it is light brown, stirring occasionally. Add celery and garlic; Sauté for 2 minutes. Add ketchup and pepper; Cook dinner 1 minute, stirring to coat. Add stock combination to pan; To a boil. Cook for 2 minutes or until the liquid is slightly thick. Add cooked tofu; Toss. Top with green onions.

Lentil-Tahini Burgers Spicy

Ingredients

- 2 cups thin purple cabbage chopped (about an ounce of 5 ½.)
- 3 tablespoons red wine vinegar
- 3/4 teaspoon kosher salt, divided
- 1 tablespoon sesame seeds
- 4 tablespoons olive oil, divided

- 1 / 2 cups finely chopped yellow onion
- 1/4 cup tahini (sesame seed paste), well shaken and
- 1/2 teaspoon ground cumin
- 1/2 teaspoon black pepper
- 8 oz. Pre-cooked lentils (about 1 1/3 cups)
- 1/2 cup grated carrots
- 1/4 cup chopped clean Cetaphil
- 3 tablespoons plain 2% low-fat Greek yogurt
- 2 tablespoons sparkling lemon juice
- 1/2 small Garlic cloves, grated
- 2 tablespoons water
- 4. (1 1/2-oz.) Whole-wheat hamburger buns, toast

Instructions

- Mix cabbage, vinegar, and half a teaspoon of salt in a bowl; Let stand for 20 minutes. drain; Stir in sesame seeds.
- Heat 1 teaspoon of oil in a pan on medium-high. Add onion; Sauté for 3 minutes.
- Place the last 1/4 teaspoon salt, 2 tablespoons tahini, cumin, black pepper and lentils in a mini food processor; Pulse 4 to 5 examples or coarsely chopped. In a bowl, mix the cooked onion, lentil mixture, carrot, and Cetaphil. Divide and divide the lentil mixture into four patties (3 ounces each).

- Heat 1 tbsp of oil in a pan on medium-high, close it. Add patties; Cook dinner for four minutes on each side.
- In a bowl, mix the remaining 2 tablespoons of tahini, yogurt, juice, and garlic. Stir in water, 1 teaspoon at a time, until the sauce reaches the desired consistency. Spread the yogurt mixture on the cut sides of the buns; Top, bottom half with the top half of patties, cabbage, and buns.

Easy Gregory Burger

Ingredients

- 1 cup cooked brown rice *
- 1 cup raw walnuts (or sub bread)
- 1/2 tbsp avocado oil (extra to cook)

- pieces 1/2 medium white onion (finely dried / half of the onion) Yield ~ 3 /) 4 cups)
- 1 tablespoon har chili powder, cumin powder, and smoked paprika
- 1/2 tsp every sea salt and pepper (more for coating burgers)
- 1 tbsp sugar (or sub natural brown or muscovado sugar)
- 1 1/2 cups cooked black beans * (well soaked, dried and dry)
- baked 1/3 cup panko bread crumbs (if using gluten-free, gluten-free bread crumbs) of vegan
- 3-4 tablespoons BBQ sauce

Instructions

- If any brown rice has not been cooked yet. Start there, by following this approach for pleasant results. Otherwise, proceed to the next step.
- Heat the pan over medium heat. Once warm, add raw walnuts and toast for 5-7 minutes, often until fragrant and golden brown. Let cool and pass to the next step.
- Meanwhile, heat the skewer evenly over medium heat. Add oil and onion as it warms up. Season with salt and pepper and sauce for 3-4 minutes, or until the onion is fragrant, soft and translucent. Remove from heat and set aside.

- Once the walnuts have cooled, mix in a blender or food processor with chili powder, cumin, smoked paprika, salt, pepper, and coconut sugar and combo until a pleasant meal () is achieved.
- In a large mixing bowl, add dried, dried black beans and mash well with a fork, leaving only a few beans ().
- Next, mix cooked rice, spice-nut mixture, onions, Panko bread crumbs, BBQ sauce and mix with a wooden spoon for 1-2 minutes or until moldable dough forms. If dry, add an additional 1-2 tablespoons (the amount is written as a unique recipe // if batch size changes by changing) BBQ sauce. Add extra Pancho bread crumbs when very wet. Taste and adjust seasonings as needed.

- For larger burgers, divide into 5 patties (1/2 cup in size // amount written as a unique recipe), or 10 smaller burgers in size (1/4 cup in size // unique recipe written). To help make patties, line your half or 1/4 measuring cup with plastic wrap and pack with the burger mixture. Press down firmly to pack, then pull out through the edge of the plastic wrap, and barely flatten with the arms to form a 3/4-inch-thick patty. Set on a baking sheet or plate for grilling.

- If grilling, heat the grill at this time and brush the grill surface with oil to make cooking easier. Otherwise, you heat the same pan used in preheated to medium heat.

- Once the skillet is hot, add just enough oil to coat the back of your skillet lightly, then add your burgers - just as easily as you would find in the pan. Otherwise, add the burger to the grill and close the lid.

- Cook for 3-4 minutes or until gently browned on the underside, turning gently. They are not as affiliated as meat burgers, although they will certainly hold their shape. Reduce heat if cooking/browning is too quick — Cook for 3-4 minutes on a separate side.

- Remove the burger from the heat to cool slightly, and at this time, but any other toppings/sides together (such as grilling / toasting your buns).

- Serve burgers or toast buns with favorite toppings. The evaporator is kept in the refrigerator for 2-3 days. See the note for freezing/heating instructions.

Best Vegan Gluten-Free Mac 'N' Cheese

Ingredients

- 1 head roasted garlic
- 10-12 ounces' gluten-free pen * (discovered at I Bionaturae pole, Whole Foods)
- 4 tablespoons olive or grapeseed oil

- 4 cloves garlic, minced Made (4 cloves) yield ~ 2 tbsp)
- 4 ½ tsp arrowroot starch *
- 2 cups plain almond milk (more as needed)
- unsweetened~ 1/4 tsp each sea salt and pepper (to taste)
- 5 tbsp dietary yeast (More to taste):
- 1/2 cup vegetarian paneer cheese (Maximal to serve)

Instructions

- To roast the garlic, preheat the oven to 400 F (204 C) and cut off the top of the garlic. Drizzle the top with a little oil, a sprinkle of salt, and wrap loosely in foil.
- Place on the oven rack without delay and roast for forty-five minutes - 1 hour depending on the dimension of garlic. You will be aware of this when garlic is very fragrant, and the bulb is golden brown. Remove from the oven, open slightly, and let cool.
- At the 40-minute mark, add about 10 cups (2400 ml // use more or less if batch size changes) to a boil over a large pot and salt liberally. After boiling, add pasta and shake to prevent the noodles from sticking. Cook according to bundle guidelines (usually about 8–10 minutes). Once fully cooked, drain and set aside.

- Meanwhile, start taking the prepared sauce. Heat a large, oven-safe pan over medium heat. When hot, add oil and minced sparkling garlic. Stir and cook for dinner for 1-2 minutes or until light golden brown. Immediately add arrowroot starch and whisk - cook dinner for 1 minute.

- Slowly add the almond milk, then prepare dinner for 2 minutes on medium heat, stirring often. The sauce will likely look a bit thicker - that's fine! We are going to combine it.

- Transfer the combination to a blender with roasted garlic. To remove the garlic, push it completely off the base, and the soft cloves need to come out correctly - so satisfying (and delicious).

- Then add salt and pepper, nutritional yeast, and vegetarian cheese and combo, scrape the side down until it becomes creamy and smooth.

- Taste and control seasonings according to taste - you especially like it salted + chutney, so don't get shy with diet yeast, salt, and vegetarian cheese.

- Return the sauce from the past to the skillet and prepare dinner over low heat until it becomes hot and thickens slightly - about 2-3 minutes - occasionally. As it heats the lower part of the back, it will become thicker and will achieve fantastic tabs (). For a thick sauce, go as far.

- To dilute slightly, add 1 tablespoon of almond milk at a time until the preferred consistency is achieved. Turn off the heat if it starts developing too aggressively.
- Add the cooked, dry pasta to the sauce and toss to coat. Then top with 1 more tablespoon vegetarian cheese (amount as a unique recipe // change in batch size if regulated).

- Optional: Heat the oven in a high oven and position a rack at the crest of the oven. Pasta over excessive pasta for 1-2 minutes (optional), or until golden brown (). Watch carefully as it can burn quickly.
- Serve immediately. I like topping mine with more pinches of vegetarian cheese - I can't get that stuff in any way.
- The evaporator retains the blanket in the refrigerator for 3 days, although fine when fresh. Heat in the microwave or on the stovetop - add almond milk if it is dry.

Sprouted Lentils

Ingredients

- 1 bowl Coconut Curried Golden Dal
- Potato
- 1 Large Candy Potato (cut into round or small wedges // on pores and skin // naturally when possible)
- 2 Tbsp Coconut or Avocado Oil
- / 4 teaspoon sea salt
- Cauliflower Rice

- 1 head cauliflower (grated in "rice" / or sub-cooked white or brown rice)
- 1 tbsp oil or water
- 1 pinch sea salt
- 1/2 teaspoon curry powder (optional)
- burn
- 1 bundle organic by kale or Collard veggies (sliced // or different beat // optional, my coconut curry Keep greens together)
- Vakalpiklia
- 1 batch Savings Cilantro sauce
- finely chopped pink cabbage chopped
- fresh cilantro
- lime leaf

Instructions

- coconut curry c Prepare a batch of Len pulses (off not cover cooking) time of dinner).
- Preheat the oven to 375 level F (190 C) and line a baking sheet with parchment paper.
- Add candy potatoes, oil *, and salt and toss to combine — Bake for 20-25 minutes or until tender and slightly brown at the ends.

- Meanwhile, keep the cabbage rice together to heat a large pan over medium heat. When hot, add oil or water, cauliflower rice, salt, and curry powder. Stir to combine.

- Reduce heat to low and heat for 3-5 minutes, masking it to enable it to steam and occasionally stirring — taste and change taste as needed.

- Next, prepare a banana with half an inch of water by heating a chopped pot or pot with extreme warmth. Bring to a boil. Then a steamer basket over the vicinity. Add bananas and cover. Steam for 2-3 minutes or wilted and shiny green remove from the pot and set aside.

- Finally, present any last serving items, such as chutney, chopped cabbage, or cilantro (all optional).

- Divide the sweet potato, dal, cabbage rice, bananas, and any additional items between the serving bowl and the bliss. Best when fresh. Store leftovers in the refrigerator for 3-4 days at a time.

Jamaican Jerk Grilled Eggplant

Ingredients

- Eggplant
- 1 teaspoon flour Cinnamon
- 1 Karachi Coriander
- 1/4 teaspoon allspice
- 1/4 teaspoon red chili
- 1/2 Every sea salt and black pepper Spinach Fresh
- 2 Karachi Thyme
- 4 cloves Garlic, minced (~ 2 Karachi minced garlic per 4 cloves)

- 1 tbsp fresh grated ginger
- 3 tbsp lemon juice
- 1/4 cup cupro or coconut amino (or GF if soy sauce is no longer)
- 2-3 tbsp sugar or maple syrup (more to taste)
- 2 big f Mc coconut oil. (Or grapeseed or avocado oil // plus more for grilling)
- 3 stalks onions or scallions (thinly sliced) naive
- 1 medium Serrano or Habanero pepper (thinly sliced // seed extracted)
- 1 large eggplant (or sub 2 1 larger 1)
- optional
- sauce 1/4 cup vegetarian BBQ sauce (I like Annie)
- 1 tbsp lemon juice
- 1 tbsp grapeseed or olive oil
- 1 tbsp coconut or maple syrup
- 1 tsp sparkling grated ginger
- 1 pinch Even Drei salt and pepper
- 1 stalk naive onion (sliced thin) chopped)
- 1 pinch Cayenne pepper (optional)

Instructions

- A short mile Mending Bowl, collectively cinnamon, coriander, all spices, cayenne, salt, pepper, thyme, garlic, ginger, lemon juice, tamarind, coconut sugar, coconut oil, green onions and flakes, and serrano / Add Habano chili.

- Taste as needed, modify taste, maximal copper for salt, lime juice for acidity, gleaming herbs for an earthy flavor, coconut sugar for sweetness, black pepper for heat, or for chewing/zing Garlic.

- Cut the eggplants vertically (in length) into a 1/2-inch-thick "steak" and brush each side generously.

- Heat a grill or grill pan to medium-high heat and gently grease/grease to discourage the eggplant from sticking. Once hot, add eggplants and grill on each strand until golden browns and grill marks are present - about 3-5 minutes on each side.

- Meanwhile, mix the sauce (optional!) Together with BBQ sauce, lime juice, oil, coconut sugar/maple syrup, ginger, salt, pepper, onion, and a little black pepper. Regulate and regulate taste to taste, including more lime for acidity, coconut sugar for sweetness, cayenne for heat, or salt for salt.

- Serve grilled eggplants over rice or with cauliflower rice or with a sauce (optional) and garnish with gleaming herbs, such as parsley or green onions. Best when fresh! The evaporator will not correct as fresh, although they will keep in the refrigerator for 2-3 days.

Noodle-Free Pad Thai

Ingredients

- 1/2 cup extra-firm tofu (extra liquid pressed, with a fork)
- crushed1 tbsp coconut pumpkin (or GF1 / 1 if not tamarind or soy sauce)
- 1 tsp chili Garlic Sauce (or 8 tsp Pink Paper Flake as a unique recipe)
- 1/4 tsp Powdered Turmeric (optional)
- Sauce
- 2 1/2 Tsp Walnut Butter (Almond Butter, Peanut Butter, Sunflower Seed Butter, etc.)

- 3 tsp Lime
- 3 1 / 2 Tbsp of coconut Amino (or sub tamari or soy sauce if no longer GF // more to taste)
- 1/2 teaspoon purple chili flake (or sub 1 teaspoon chili garlic sauce - Huy Fong Foods brand)
- 1 tbsp maple syrup (12) G coconut sugar // extra to taste)
- Veggies
- 1 tbsp sesame oil (sub-water or leave if low / no-fat)
- 1 medium serrano pepper (seed + stem extracted, finely chopped // Leave for less heat)
- 1 small bundle inexperienced onion (Ends + thinly sliced)
- 1 1/2 cups finely chopped crimson cabbage
- 1 medium crimson bell pepper (cored and thinly sliced length)
- 2 tbsp coconut amino nos (or tamari or soy sauce if gluten-free // Not Divided)
- 4-5 mass carrots (peeled with vegetable peel and packed with ribbons // ~ 4 cups)
- 6 leaves collard greens (large stems removed; stacked / finely chopped // ~ 2 cup filled)
- was 1/2 teaspoon grated Other (Optional // or 1/4 teaspoon ground ginger as a written authentic recipe)
- 1/2 teaspoon turmeric (the grated Alternatively // or 1/4 teaspoon turmeric floor)
- serves to alternate

- fresh cilantro
- crushed peanuts/peanut sauce,
- red pepper flake

Instructions

- that serve with tofu: tofu is a small mixing bowl and coconut amino from, chili garlic sauce (Or pepper layer), and turmeric (optional) That I am not in the series of books. Stir and set aside.
- Combine all the sauce ingredients in a small mixing bowl and whisk to combine. Taste and regulated taste as needed, more lemon juice for acidity, coconut amino for salt, red chili flake or chili sauce for summer, or maple syrup for sweetness.
- Heat a large pan over medium heat. Once heated, add oil (or water), black pepper, onion, cabbage, bell pepper, and half of the coconut amino to veggies (1 tbsp is written as a unique recipe). Cook for 3 minutes, stirring/bouncing repeatedly.

- Pour the tofu into a nook of the pan and fry until slightly brown, often stirring - about 3-5 minutes.
- Add the carrots and collard veggies, and the remaining half of the coconut to the veggies (1 tbsp is written as a unique

recipe) and stir. Sauté for 2 minutes. Then add Pad Thai sauce and freshly grated ginger and turmeric (optional).

- Sauté on medium heat through and through the warmer are slightly wilted - about 3 minutes - stirring often.
- Taste and adjust the dish to taste as needed, add extra maple syrup for sweetness, red chili flake or chili garlic for summer, coconut amino for salt, or lime juice for acidity.
- Divide between serving plates and enjoy. Serve with peanut sauce, crushed peanuts, Cetaphil, and lime wedges. 2 functions as a side or 4 as an entry.

Moroccan Lentil-Stuffed Eggplant

Ingredients

- Eggplant
- 4 small eggplants
- 2 tbsp avocado or coconut oil (if oil, keep sub water off)
- 1 pinch sea salt
- LentILS /
- batch pickled lentils
- 1 3/4 cups beaten tomatoes (crushed first Rate) flavor and texture // dipped or cooked tomatoes)

- 1/4 tsp each sea salt and pepper (more to taste)
- 1/2 tsp smoked paprika (larger to taste)
- TOPPING
- 1 1/2 teaspoon gluten-free panko bread crumbs (I like Ian's company panko bread crumbs)
- for serving optional
- freshly chopped parsley coriander
- white or brown rice or cauliflower rice

Instructions

- Preheat oven to 375 degrees Fahrenheit (190 C) and a 9x13 exit -inch (or similar size) baking dish.
- In a large saucepan or Rimmel skillet, mix Moroccan-spiced lentils, overwhelmed tomatoes, salt, pepper, and paprika. Heat on medium heat till bubbling. Then reduce the boil to a minimum and prepare dinner for 5 minutes. Regulate the taste for flavor and mix more salt and pepper to taste in general, or paprika for smokey.
- Watch the eggplants thin and roll. Otherwise, use a knife to cut an angular split from the core of your eggplant. Then use a spoon to scrape a hollow center. Leave enough brinjal meat to hold the lentils (). (Save the leftover brinjal to make things like brinjal curry, Persian brinjal dip or baba Ganesh.) chopped

- Heat a large skillet over medium heat. Once heated, pour the oil and eggplant cut-side down and cover - you may have to do these two (or more if increasing the batch size) depending on the size of your pan. Cook on one side for 4-5 minutes or until barely baked. Then flip the brinjals aside, cover, and prepare dinner for 4-5 minutes. You are looking for the eggplant to soften and brown on the outside.

- After the eggplants are cooked, cut-side up in your baking dish, and top with the lentils, there should be plenty to fill the eggplants and some overflow, which can be spooned down into the dish. Top with vegetarian Parmesan cheese and Panko bread crumbs.
- The brinjal is baked for 30–35 minutes or until the eggplant is soft and brown, and the lentils are boiled. Bread crumbs are browned.
- Serve as rice or cauliflower rice (optional). Garnish with fresh parsley or cilantro (optional) for color and flavor.
- Best when fresh, although leftovers are stored in the fridge for four days or in the freezer for up to 1 month.

Garlic and White Wine Paste

Ingredients

- Brussels sprouts 16 ounces Brussels (half)
- 1-2 tablespoons olive oil
- 1 pinch every sea salt + use pepper
- paste 3 tablespoons olive oil or vegan butter

- 4 large cloves Garlic, sliced (yield) ~ 3 Tbsp. as a written unique recipe)
- 1/3 cup dry white wine (Pinot Gorgio, Chardonnay, + Sauvignon Blanc, are the best)
- 4 Tbsp. arrowroot starch (or cornstarch)
- 1 3 / 4 cup unsweetened Undisturbed Almond Milk
- 4 Tbsp. Nutritional Yeast
- Sea Salt + Black Pepper Taste
- 1/4 Cup Vegetarian Parmesan Cheese (more to serve)
- 10 oz Vegetarian, Gluten-Free Pasta * (Brown Rice Pasta Easily Handed - or Bionetgen Pen)
- garlic bread *
- simple inexperienced salad *

Instructions

- Preheat the oven to 400 levels F (204 C) and stir Brussels sprouts on a baking sheet (if meeting So an increase in the size and use of the baking sheet). Drizzle with oil and season liberally with salt and pepper and toss. Arrange in a layer and set aside.
- Bring a large pot of water to boil (to cook pasta) and generously salt (~ 1 tbsp.). Set aside while preparing the sauce.
- Heat a large rimmed pan over medium heat. When hot, add oil and garlic. Sauté for 3 minutes or until fragrant and

very hard golden brown, then add wine (). Be careful - it can also flame, though only briefly. Stir and sauté for 2–4 minutes, or until the wine reduces with the aid of about half.

- Add arrowroot and whisk, then add almond milk and whisk. At this point, it would be very bad - this is normal. Transfer to a high-speed blender and add nutritional yeast, salt + pepper, and vegan cheese. Blend on excessively until creamy and smooth.

- Taste and modify the flavor as needed, adding more vegetarian Parmesan or dietary yeast for a more delicious flavor, or salt and pepper for a universal flavor.

- Transfer the sauce back to the skillet and heat it to medium-low heat while stirring. The sauce becomes thick, at which point you can reduce the pasta until it is hot and the pasta can boil until cooked. If it looks too thick, thin with almond milk, if too thin, it increases the heat to medium to induce thickening.

- Add the Brussels sprouts to the oven and prepare dinner for 12–15 minutes or until slightly golden brown and tender at the 10–15-minute mark to induce cooking.

- Around this time, pour pasta into boiling water and cook according to bundle instructions (mine was about 7-10 minutes, so they did. You want to execute pasta and Brussels with the same amount of time).

- Once cooked, the pasta is dried and once added to the sauce, mixed with half of the Brussels, and tossed for a combination. Season with a little extra vegetarian paneer (optional) for added flavor.
- Serve with the ultimate Brussels sprouts and extra vegetarian Parmesan cheese to taste. I also like a bit of Crimson Paper Flake, although this is optional.
- Best when fresh, even if left well in the refrigerator for 2-3 days. Heat in the microwave for best results.

Baked Quinoa Black Beans Fruit Fil Quinoa

Ingredients

- 1 cup cooked and cooled (make sure it is cooked and definitely cooled before use)
- 1 15-ounce black beans (rinsed, dried, drained)
- 1/5 cup pumpkin seeds (raw or roasted)
- 5 cloves garlic (skin wipe and crushed)
- 1/2 teaspoon sea salt, plus to taste
- 1 tsp cumin seeds
- 1/2 tsp coriander

- 2 tablespoons tomato paste
- 2 The Big Mac
- Malabar nut 1 Chipotle pepper (less spicy Otit for Falafel) into the sauce
- 1 teaspoon dietary yeast (optional)

Instructions

- if you have not yet your quinoa, it's time to do (Make positive it is cooked and is absolutely cold before use).
- Preheat the oven to 350 degrees F (176 C), add rinsed, dried black beans to the parchment-lined baking sheet. Cracks appear for 15 minutes or until the beans are dry and feel dry to the touch. Remove the beans from the oven and then increase the heat of the oven to 375 tier F (190 C).
- Add the black beans in a food processor along with the pumpkin seeds and garlic and the pulses to an unexpected meal. Then add cooked/cooled quinoa, salt, cumin, coriander, tomato paste, coconut amino, chipotle pepper in adobo, and diet yeast (optional). Blend to combine until a textured dough forms (you are not searching for puree).
- Regulate the taste as needed, including flavor for flavor, depth of flavor, coconut sauce for flavor, adobo sauce for heat, cumin for a smoothie, or salt for overall flavor.
- Scoop 1 1/2 tablespoons volume (using this scoop or a tablespoon) and gently structure into small discs using

your hands. Add fashioned falafel to a parchment-lined baking sheet.

- Bake for 15 minutes. Then flip for additional baking or baking for 10–15 minutes or until golden brown and crisp on the edges.
- These are delicious with Falafel Hummus, Garlic Dill Sauce, Baba Ganesh, or Tahini Sauce. For extra heat, try garnishing with chili garlic sauce. Serve on greens or beaten, or enjoy as is!
- Store the remaining pieces in the refrigerator for 3-4 days. To freeze, either bake once and refrigerate or freeze before baking. Then add to a freezer-safe container and freeze for 1 month. Heat in a 375 diploma F (190 C) oven until heated.

Thai Yellow Coconut Curry Mango

Ingredients

- Curry
- 1½ (or avocado or grapeseed oil) of coconut oil
- 1 medium onion, minced
- 2 Karachi minced sparkling ginger
- 2 cloves minced garlic (2 cloves yield ~ 1 tablespoon)
- Or 1 Thai red pepper (Serrano pepper // stem removed and finely chopped with seeds)

- 1 cup chopped red cabbage (optional)
- 3 tablespoons pink curry paste *
- 2 14-ounce cans of light coconut milk (Sub 1 max Light 2 cans full fat per fat texture)
- more than sugar (to taste 3 Tbsp coconut)
- 1/4 tsp sea salt (more to taste)
- 2-3 tsp tamari (or soy sauce if not gluten-free)
- 1 tsp ground turmeric removed
- 1 red bell pepper (seeds and stem) / cut into bite-size pieces)
- 1/4 cup naive peas (optional // frozen or fresh)
- 2 ripe mangos
- 1/4 cup roasted cashew nuts (salted) Just an, i.e., security)
- 1 Middle somewhere or not land,
- the area per global Kalpika juice
- leaf
- (lemon Thai or regular)) Basil, or sparkling coriander, for
- brown rice serving * or coconut quinoa
- steam broccoli

Instructions

- Heat a large forged iron or steel pan with an excessive rim over medium heat. When hot, add coconut oil, dry ginger, ginger, garlic, and black pepper. Add sea salt and a pinch of sautéing for 2-3 minutes, stirring often.

- Add cabbage (optional) and pink curry paste and shake, and cook dinner for another 2 minutes.

- Add coconut milk, coconut sugar, sea salt, tamarind, turmeric, and stir. Bring to a boil over medium heat.
- Once boiling, add pink chili and peas (optional) and reduce heat to low. You want a boil, no longer boil, which should be round to medium to low heat.
- Cook for 5–10 minutes, occasionally stirring, to soften pepper and peas, and infect them with curry flavor.
- At this time, add additional flavor and modify the flavor of the broth as needed. I offered more coconut sugar for sweetness, tamari and sea salt for salt, and turmeric for the earth. You can add extra spices for a spicier and highly curry flavor. Don't be shy with spices - this curry will be very tasty.
- Once the broth is properly sewn, and the chili becomes soft, add the mango, cashew, and lemon juice, and boil on low to medium heat for 3-4 minutes.
- Serve rice or coconut quinoa, or boiled broccoli (broccoli being my favorite). This dish is multiplied with more lemon juice and Thai or regular bas

The Best Vegetarian 'Full Pork' Sandwich

Ingredients

- Lentils
- 2 cups of water
- 1 cup inexperienced lentils (well rinsed)
- spices / carrots
- 2 Karachi olive or grapeseed oil

- 1/2 medium white or yellow onion (minced // to serve plus More)
- / grated carrot 1 ½ cup finely chopped pack (I used the attachment of my food processor)
- 2 teaspoons coconut sugar or natural brown sugar (more to taste)
- 1 half teaspoon ground
- turnips 1 teaspoon garlic powder
- 1 S Healthy pinch each sea salt + black pepper (more to taste)
- 3/4-gram vegetarian BBQ sauce (plus more to serve // I used Annie's Authentic BBQ Sauce)
- 2karachi water
- to serve
- medium sizes 4Gluten-free or wheat hamburger buns *
- Finely chopped red cabbage, carrots, and green onions (optional)

Instructions

- To make a small saucepan, add water and rinsed lentils and heat over medium-high heat. Bring to a low boil, then reduce heat to a boil and cook uncovered for about 18 minutes, or until tender. There should be a regular boil in water (not boiling). Turn off any excess liquid and set aside.

- When the lentils are almost cooked, heat a large pan on medium heat. Once hot, add oil and onion and season with a pinch of salt and pepper (an amount is written as a batch recipe // adjust if batch size changes). Stir to combine, and sauté for 4-5 minutes, stirring often, or until onions are tender and slightly brown.

- Then add cooked lentils, carrots, coconut sugar, paprika, garlic powder, salt, pepper, and beef sauce (). Stir to combine.

- Continue baking the mixture over medium-low heat until completely heated and thickened, shake now and again - about 5–10 minutes.

- Regulating the taste according to taste and adding more paprika to the taste, adding salt to salt, coconut sugar for sweetness, or BBQ sauce for depth of flavor.

- Optional: Put half of the mixture in a food processor and (using an "S" formed blade) to mash together some mixture of lentils/carrots. It creates a more comfortable texture, which I like.

- Serve the mixture on toasted buns with toppings of choice. I went with sliced crimson cabbage, carrots, and sliced inexperienced onions. Serve with more BBQ sauce for more flavor.

- Best when fresh, although the lentil mixture will remain in the fridge for up to three days. If the combination is dry, heat it in the microwave or through hot water on the stovetop.

Crispy Gluten-Free Eggplant Parmesan

Ingredients

- 1/2 cup Sweet Plain Almond Milk (or other neutral dairy-free milk)
- 1 tsp Cornstarch (or arrowroot starch)
- Flour Coating
- 1/2 cup Gluten-Free Flour
- 2 Karachi Cornstarch (or arrowroot starch)

- 1 healthy Chutki sea salt
- Dry coating
- 1/3 cup gluten-free bread Panco Crumbs * (I prefer this brand)
- 1/4 cup cornmeal
- 1/4 cup vegetarian Prmans cheese
- 1 teaspoon Oregano as Ti *
- 1/4 teaspoon sea salt
- Eggplant
- 1 full length, the slender eggplant (1/8-inch shells // holes and chopped skin)
- 4 tablespoons cooking oil (Avocado or Coconut //)
- for optional
- Split Me1 cup easy marinara sauce (or your favorite store offered) sauce serving)
- 8-10 oz. Cooked Pasta (such as Linguini, Pen, or Spiralizer Vegetables) Heat the
- 1 batch 30-minute Cashew Alfredo Sauce

Instruction

- oven to four hundred levels F (204 C) and line a baking sheet with parchment paper. Also, in a bowl collectively pour almond milk and cornstarch to your dipping stations; In another bowl, gluten-free flour, cornstarch, and sea salt; And gluten-free Panco bread crumbs, cornmeal, vegetarian Parmesan cheese, parsley, and sea salt in some other bowls ().

- If served with pasta and sauce, prepare this time (optional). Once pasta is cooked, drain and cover with a towel to keep it warm.
- Next, dip the eggplant slices into the flour mixture, then the almond milk mixture and then the breadcrumbs and arrange the rounds dipped on a smooth plate.
- Heat a large pan over medium heat. When heated, add 2 tablespoons of oil (30 mL // as the recipe is written, add/adjust if changing batch size). Allow the oil to warm for 1 minute. Then add 4-5 eggplant shells at a time and brown it for 2-3 minutes on each side or until it turns light golden brown. Then add to the prepared baking sheet, and add the baking sheet to the oven so that the eggplants can begin baking.
- Fry the bringing in the brinjals until all the rounds have turned brown and continue in the oven if the pan contains too much oil to cook, brown the brinjals too quickly.
- Bake the eggplants for 10-15 minutes or until they are crispy and golden brown, making sure to bake as soon as you turn in between. Serve with favorite facets and sauces.
- I like to dabble in my cashew alfredo and serve my eggplant parmesan with a marinara sauce for gluten-free

pasta! (For more aspects and chutney options, test the selection in the above publication.)

- Best when fresh. But you can store the leftover eggplants covered in the fridge for up to 2 days. Heat on a baking sheet in a 350-degree F (176 C) oven until heated

Garlic Sandwich Potato Noodle Pasta Unripe

Ingredients

- 1 cup cashews
- 3 cloves garlic (mix for added or less flavor to the preferred garlic flavor) Dietrich Spoon
- 4-5 tablespoons sea salt
- 2 arrowroot starch (or cornstarch) to thicken.
- 1 1/2 - 2 cups uncooked almonds or rice milk, +as much as possible
- 1 pinch pink pepper flake (optional for less spicy)
- overcooked noodles

- 3 medium sweet potato (when possible, peeled and Served Spiral *)
- optional for
- Fresh chopped parsley
- Sautéed kale or Kale Chips
- Crispy chickpea (store sold or DIY)
- Vegan Parmesan Cheese Pour
- Red Chili Flake

Instructions

- Cashews into a small mixing bowl and let cows in very hot water for 30 minutes Insert Then drain completely and set aside. (Or soak cashew nuts in cold water overnight or 6-8 hours)
- If served with banana chips or step bananas (or crispy chickpeas), prepare now and set aside until serving.
- While the cashews finish soaking, peel and slice the potatoes using a veggie spiralizer. Or if you don't personalize a spiralizer, you can use a vegetable peeler or julienne peeler instead.
- Add soaked and dry cashews to a high-speed blender. Then add the closing ingredients: garlic, dietary yeast, salt, arrowroot starch, and almond or rice milk.
- Whisk until creamy and smooth, rub down as needed. Taste / regulate as needed, add extra garlic for zing/kick,

add nutritional yeast for "shininess," salt for salt, or a pinch of red chili flake (optional) for heat. The sauce should be creamy, smooth and smooth. If too thick, with a little extra almond milk.

- Transfer the sauce to a large, rim pan or pot and heat over medium-low heat until it just starts to bubble. The warmer it is, the thicker it is. Conductors limit warmness to a very low boil once the heat is maintained. The sauce will thicken, so dilute it with additional almonds or rice milk as needed.

- Pour 1 inch of water into a huge pot and top with a steamer basket (if you don't have a steamer basket, books). Heat over medium-high heat and add potato noodles as your bubble. Cover to steam for 3-5 minutes or until al dente or slightly softened (depending on taste). Be careful not to steam too long, or noodles can become disgusting.

- Add your candy potatoes to your sauce and toss gently to combine. If adding Kel or other add-ins, add this time.
- Serve or garnish with fresh parsley, crunchy chickpeas, bananas, vegetarian gravy, or red chili flake (optional).
- This dish is first-rate when fresh, as the noodles are swollen after heating, but the taste is still delicious! If storing for later, I recommend retaining the banana and other toppings separately. I will preserve it in the

refrigerator for three days — heat on the stovetop or microwave.

Collard Green Spring Rolls + Sunbutter Dipping Saving Blundered Ward Veggies

Ingredients

- 10 oz Extra-firm Tofu * (optional for brushing with rolls in sesame)
- 1 (~ 11-12 large collars per bundle)
- 1 small Crimson Bell Peppers (black pepper) finely sliced vertically)

- 1 ½ cups bean sprouts
- 1 cup packed basil
- 1 cup chopped crimson (purple) cabbage
- 3 medium whole carrots (peel and very finely chopped // I used my Mandolin Mead With teeth through blade)
- Sauce
- 1/3 cup creamy unsalted sunflowers seed butter
- 1 1/2 -2 tablespoons Trim (Or soy sauce if no longer GF)
- 2-3 tablespoons maple syrup (to taste)
- 1/2 medium lime, juice (yield ~ 2 tablespoons or 30 ml) written as an original recipe)
- 1/2 tsp chili Garlic Sauce (or 1 Thai Purple Chili Minced // or 1/4 Tsp Powdered Black Pepper Flake
- hot water (to thin)

Instructions

- Use tofu wrapped in a clean, absorbent towel to wipe off excess li and setting something heavy (such as a cast-iron skillet) on the top is Rs.
- Meanwhile, prepare the greens by cutting the stems and cutting them, using a small, sharp knife, to reduce the thickness of the stems at the base of the leaf. This is not always an important step, although it will allow it to bend/roll with extra ease.

- Next, prepare the great and cut the tofu into long, rectangular cubes. Arrange on a tray or slicing board.

- Prepare dipping sauce with the help of sunflower seed butter, tamarind, maple syrup, lime juice, and chili garlic sauce and mix in a small mixing bowl. Add warm water diluted to a thick but thin sauce. Taste and modify as needed, including additional lime juice for acidity, chili garlic sauce for heat, maple syrup for sweetness, or tamari for salt.

- Next, lay a green spatula on the flat surface, and near the stem, layer on the basil, tofu, crimson pepper, cabbage, bean sprout, and carrot (). Use collard green to bend into your arms as soon as the stuffing is secured from the inside, and then tuck in the aspects of collard green and continue rolling until you have an unexpected spring roll. Lie seam-side up on the serving platter and continue until all the filler is used - about 11-12 rolls (as an authentic recipe // modify the amount // if batch size changes).

- To serve, I sliced my rolls into 1/2 and arranged them in a serving bowl with dipping sauce (). But you can additionally just complete them!

- These stay exceptionally well in the refrigerator for 3 days, and the sauce will last for 5-7 days.

Mediterranean Baked Sweet Potatoes

Ingredients

- 4 media (~ lb. each) candy potatoes *
- 1 15-ounce chickpea (rinse and dry)
- 1/31/2 tbsp olive

- 1/2 teaspoon each cumin, coriander, cinnamon, smoked (or regularly), Paprika
- 1 pinch of sea salt or lemon juice (optional)
- Girley Hard Cues hummus
- 1/4 cup (or tahini)
- 1/2 medium lemon, juice (1/2 lemon yield ~ 1 tbsp juice)
- 3/4 - 1 tsp dried dill (or sub 2-3 tablespoons clear 3 / 4-1 teaspoon dried)
- 3 cloves garlic, minced (3 cloves yield ~ 1 half Mm or 9 grams)
- water or soaked in almond milk without (to thin)
- sea salt to taste (Optional) / I didn't need any)
- Toppings Optional
- 1/4 cup cherry tomatoes (diced)
- 1/4 cup chopped parsley (minced)
- 2 tablespoons lemon juice
- chili garlic sauce

Instructions

- Oven range to four hundred f (204 C) and heat in line. Huge baking sheet with foil.
- Scrub the potatoes and cut them in half lengthwise. This will speed up the cooking time. Otherwise, go completely and bake for a long time (approximately twice the time (45 minutes - 1 hour).

- Remove the peeled and dried peel with olive oil and spices and place it on a foil-lined baking sheet. Rub with olive oil and face the area on the same baking sheet (or another baking sheet depending on the size).

- While the candy potatoes and chickpeas are frying, combine all the components in a mixing bowl. Pour your sauce together to whisk and whisper for a combination, including just enough water to dilute almond milk. So, it changes the flavor and as needed. Add extra garlic for maximum zing, to taste. Salt, lemon juice for freshness, and dill for an extra serious herb flavor. I wanted nothing. Other.

- Note: If you don't have hummus, then Rohini (which you DIY can!) Would make a great base replacement for the sauce - just modify the to accommodate the lack of flavor the tahini provides.

- seasonings. Also, add the parsley-tomato with the top layer of tomato with lemon juice. And by separating the parsley to bounce and marinate.

- Once the sweet potato thorns turn soft, and the chickpeas are golden brown - about 25 minutes - disposed of the oven.

- To serve, flip the potato flesh and shake the insides a little. Then peak with chickpeas, sauce, and parsley-tomato garnish. serve immediately.

- Additional key ideas may include hummus, pita chips, baba ghanoush, or Persian eggplant dip! As a pleasure!

Butternut Squash Veggie Pizza

Ingredients

Sauce

- 3 cups butternut squash (CU *)
- 3 cloves garlic (whole // pores and remove skin)
- 2 tbsp olive oil (divided)
- 1 pinch sea salt + pepper
- 1 tbsp maple syrup

- Pizza
- 1cup broccolini Half (chopped // large stems removed)
- 1/2 cup pink onion (chopped)
- 1/2 cup ripe chickpeas (fully drained and completely dry // optional)
- 1 pinch sea salt + pepper
- 1 teaspoon dried thyme
- 6 oz store-bought the pizza Interpretation (I Love Trader Joe's Garlic & Herb or whole wheat // or gluten-free recipes)
- 1 Cup butternut squash sauce (recipe above)
- 1/2 cup vegan cheese or store-bought veg mozzarella cheese * for
- serving optional
- vegetarian tasting. Cheese
- cayenne flakes

I

Instructions

- Preheat oven to 400 ranges F (204 C) and serve a rack in the middle of the oven.
- Put cubed butternut squash and peeled garlic cloves on a baking sheet and drizzle with half of the olive oil (1 tbsp written as the original recipe // adjust the batch size) and every salt and pepper. Pinch to Toss to combine.

- Bake for 15-20 minutes, or until all the squash fork is tender.
- Transfer the squash and garlic to a blender or food processor with the final olive oil (1 tbsp written/modified if changing the batch size) and maple syrup as an authentic recipe. Puree until creamy and smooth, including a touch of extra olive oil or water if it is too thick. The consistency is creamy and diffused (not pourable).
- Taste and make changes as needed.
- Heat a large pan over medium heat. When hot, add 1 tsp of oil, broccolini, onion, chickpeas (optional), salt and pepper, and parsley. Sauté for 2-3 minutes, stirring often. To cancel.
- Increase the heat of the oven to 425 F (218 C).
- Roll the pizza dough in a uniform circle and switch to a parchment-lined round baking sheet (or an object of similar size).
- Top with ~ 1 cup of sauce (you will have leftover sauce, which you can reserve for other pizzas // as the amount the original recipe wrote // regulate if change batch size), veggies, and Chickpeas. Sprinkle some more parsley and veg Parmesan cheese (or vegetarian mozzarella).

- Immediately transfer the oven to the oven, laying the pizza and parchment paper on the rack (close the baking sheet so it can bake once on the rack for a crisp crust). Bake for 13-18 minutes or until the sides of the crust are golden brown.

- Slice and serve with the ultimate Parmesan cheese, dried parsley, and cayenne flakes (optional). The leftovers hold up well for 2-3 days, although excellent when fresh.

Savory Tahini Dressing Contained Fish

Ingredients

Vegetables

- 1 medium (sliced into 1/4-inch) sliced into 1/4-inch
- 1 medium sweet potato ()

- 1 cup red cabbage (sliced)
- 1 tbsp coconut oil. Or use our method for sub-water or oil-free vegetables)
- 1 pinch sea salt
- 1/2 teaspoon DIY curry powder (or shop-bought)

Dressing

- 1/3 cup tahini
- 1/2 teaspoon garlic powder (plus to taste and More) more than
- 1 Karachi Coconut Amino (style or sub tamari or soy sauce)
- 1 pinch sea salt (if the taste is extra, skip using tamarind or soy sauce)
- 1 huge clove garlic (minced)
- 1/4~ cup of water (thin)
-

Salad

- 6 cups Mitch, whether vegetables Kill, romaine, mixed greens, etc.)
- 4 small radishes (finely chopped)
- 3 tablespoons asafetida seeds
- 1 ripe avocado ()
- (in2 tablespoons lemon Juice or Apple Cider Vinegar
- Dense Toppings Non-Essentials / Choose Your Favorite
- 1 Batch Crispy Baked Chico

- 2 Cups Cooked Quinoa * (I missed my // with quinoa curry powder to retain the grain)
- DIY Kimchi (or store-bought)

Instructions

- if quinoa or crunchy If you have six, then prepare this time. Otherwise, proceed to step 2.
- Preheat the oven to 375 ranges F (190 C) and arrange the zucchini, cabbage and sweet potatoes on a baking sheet (one or more as needed). Drizzle with coconut oil (or sub-oil-free option), sea salt and curry powder and toss to combine — Fry for 20 minutes or until soft and barely golden brown.

- Meanwhile, combine tahini, garlic powder, coconut amino, sea salt, and garlic in a small mixing bowl and make a dressing that mixes together. Then add enough water to the batter and beat until smooth. Taste and modify the seasonings to add more garlic powder for flavor, coconut amino for the depth of flavor, or salt for flavor.
- Gather the salad by adding greens, radishes, hemp seeds, and avocado to a large mixing bowl. Add lemon juice (or apple cider vinegar) and toss gently to combine.
- Add roasted greens and any other favorite toppings (quinoa, chickpeas, etc.) and serve with dressing.

- Best when fresh, even if leftovers are well left in the fridge for three days. One stored dressing at a time will be held for 7 days. The chick should be saved once at room temperature to preserve crispness.

Conclusion

Thank you for making it through to the end of Plant-Based Cookbook for Beginners, let's hope it was informative and able to provide you with all of the tools you need to achieve your goals whatever they may be.

The objective of this guide is to help you discover all the benefits and alternatives of preparing plant-based meals to easily learn how to prepare and plan healthy and balanced meals for every day of the week and to start saving time, money, calories and energy!
We also hope you will find the recipes we shared with you useful and enjoyable, on how to plan a balanced breakfast, lunch and dinner in a quick and easy way for the whole family.

Finally, if you found this book useful in any way, a review is always appreciated!

CPSIA information can be obtained
at www.ICGtesting.com
Printed in the USA
BVHW040212250521
608079BV00015B/484